新编国际经济与贸易专业系列教材

外贸函电

FOREIGN TRADE CORRESPONDENCE

（第三版）

于晓云　主编

首都经济贸易大学出版社
Capital University of Economics and Business Press
·北 京·

图书在版编目（CIP）数据

外贸函电 / 于晓云主编. -- 3 版. -- 北京 : 首都经济贸易大学出版社, 2025. 8. -- ISBN 978-7-5638-3918-6

Ⅰ. F75

中国国家版本馆 CIP 数据核字第 2025EU4809 号

外贸函电(第三版)
于晓云　主编
Waimao Handian

责任编辑　田玉春
封面设计　砚祥志远·激光照排 TEL: 010-65976003
出版发行　首都经济贸易大学出版社
地　　址　北京市朝阳区红庙(邮编 100026)
电　　话　(010)65976483　65065761　65071505(传真)
网　　址　https://sjmcb. cueb. edu. cn
经　　销　全国新华书店
照　　排　北京砚祥志远激光照排技术有限公司
印　　刷　北京建宏印刷有限公司
成品尺寸　170 毫米×240 毫米　1/16
字　　数　262 千字
印　　张　15. 5
版　　次　2015 年 4 月第 1 版　2021 年 4 月第 2 版　**2025 年 8 月第 3 版**
印　　次　2025 年 8 月总第 5 次印刷
书　　号　ISBN 978-7-5638-3918-6
定　　价　48. 00 元

前言(第三版)

随着经济全球化的不断深入,各国间的经济贸易联系日益密切。据海关统计,2024年,我国货物贸易进出口总值为43.85万亿元人民币,我国的贸易伙伴也呈现多元化的趋势,这使得外贸函电需要在内容和形式上做相应的改进。外贸函电课程作为国际经济与贸易专业的核心业务课程之一,是一门将英语与外贸业务相结合的课程,在商务英语专业、国际贸易专业和国际商务专业人才培养过程中占有重要的地位。它的作用在于培养学生熟练掌握外贸业务中常用的基本术语及表达技巧,其指导思想是培养具有外贸业务工作能力的高素质国际贸易人才。

为此,本书以 Jin Yuan 进出口公司和 Fashion General Trading Co. 公司就桑蚕丝类纺织品的交易过程为背景,帮助学生掌握进出口流程,以及往来信件中的专业词汇、常用句型。全书共分13个单元,包括商务书信的结构、写作技巧、建立业务关系、询盘、报盘、还盘、订货、支付条款、装运条款、保险、索赔等环节的书信。其中,我们应重点关注建立业务关系、询盘、报盘、还盘、订货信的写作。每单元分为以下部分:学习目标、案例导入、内容介绍、样本信、词语注释、常用表达式、练习、信件选读和扩展阅读。每单元开头提供的信件为 Jin Yuan 和 Fashion General Trading Co. 两家公司按照业务环节所撰写的商务信函，这是本书的一大特色。此外，案例导入、以电子邮件方式沟通、信件选读和扩展阅读使全书的内容更加完整，也更联系实际。

本书由于晓云编写。在编写过程中作者参阅了国内外与商务写作、贸易实务相关的书籍，在此向有关作者致以真诚的敬意。

编者

2025年5月

Contents

Chapter 1 Structure and Formats of Business Letters 商务书信的结构和格式

Learning Objectives

- Grasp the structure of a business letter
- Learn the formats of a business letter
- Master the layout of envelope for a business letter
- Have a general idea of the characteristics of fax and e-mail
- Grasp the structure of a fax
- Grasp the structure of an e-mail

学习目标：了解商务书信的结构、格式、信封的写法；对传真和电子邮件有一定认识。

Introduction

Business letter is the most frequently used form of communication in international trade. An effective business letter should state clearly and simply. If a business person is unable to write an effective business letter, it is very difficult for him/her to express his/her ideas or requests clearly.

As major business is transacted by a business letter, its importance can be recognized clearly. Along with the development of modern technology, more and more people are using the facsimile and the e-mail to transmit the formal business letters in international trade. The form of transmission may be variable, but its essence remains unchanged.

There are three formats of business communication: the blocked style, the indented style and the semi-blocked style.

Structure of Business Letter
商务书信的结构

Business letter has its special structure. Generally speaking, a business letter consists of basic parts and optional parts.

1. Basic parts 必备部分

A typical business letter usually includes seven basic parts: letterhead, date line, inside name and address, salutation, body, complimentary close and signature.

(1) Letterhead 信头

In letterhead stationery of many companies, letterhead is professionally printed at the top of the page. Of course, sometimes it may be printed at the bottom or even at the upper-left corner of the page. If letterhead stationery is not available, the addresser can type the heading, which normally comprises of the name, address, telephone, fax number, e-mail address of the company sending the letter. Sometimes a logo or corporate design can be included in the letterhead. For example:

Wanli Batteries Group Ltd.
No. 11 Zonghan Industrial Park, Cixi
Zhejiang Province, 315300, P. R. China
Tel: 0574-66540000   Fax: 0574-66540000

(2) Date 日期

The date should be typed three or four lines below the letterhead. It is typed at the centre for modified block format and flush left for block format. The date can be arranged in the order of day, month, year or month, day, year. The month should be typed in full and not abbreviated; otherwise, it may easily cause confusion. The day can be expressed in either cardinal numbers (1, 2, etc.) or in ordinal numbers (1st, 2nd, 3rd, etc.). For example, 09/03/2025 can be taken as September 3, 2025 by Americans or 9 March, 2025 by British. The date should be expressed as follows:

March 4, 2025
March 4th, 2025 (American style)
4th March, 2025 (British style)

(3) Inside Name and Address 封内地址

Normally, the inside name and address should include some or all parts of the following: the name of the addressee, the name of the department, the name of the company, room number, street address, city, postcode, state/province and country. It appears exactly the same way as that on the envelope. The inside name and address cannot be left out, as the envelope is often thrown away. Besides, the inside name and address can avoid the mistakes of putting the letter in a wrong envelope.

Mr., Mrs., Miss, and Messrs. are the courtesy titles for use on the first line of the inside address in writing to an individual. If you do not know whether a person is a man or a woman and you have no way to find out, omit the courtesy title and give the full name.

If an addressee holds a business title, the title should follow the person's name. It can be placed on the same line of the person's name or on the line below. If the title appears on the same line, place a comma between the name and the title. For example:

Mr. James Marsh, Assistant President
Or
Mr. James Marsh
Assistant President

If the name of a specific person is unavailable, the letter can be addressed to the department followed by the name of the company. For example:

Strategic Investment Department
International Trading Co., Ltd.

If the name of the company contains a person's name, the word "Messrs." is put before the name of the company to show courtesy. For example:

Messrs. Marsh Corporation

In order to avoid ambiguity, if a letter is addressed to a company in a certain country, the name of the country should be included in the inside name and address, even if the city mentioned is the capital of the country.

Of all these parts, postcode is very important. It helps to facilitate mechanical mail-sorting.

The inside name and address appears on the left margin and usually starts two to four lines below the date.

(4) Salutation 称呼

The salutation is an expression of courtesy with which a letter begins. It should be identical to the first line of the inside name and address. Its form depends on the relationship between the addresser and the addressee.

The customary formal greeting in a business letter is "Dear Sir" or "Dear Madam", used for addressing one person. "Dear Sirs" "Dear Mesdames" or "Gentlemen" are used for addressing two or more people. If the addresser knows the addressee personally, a warmer greeting such as "Dear Mr. Marsh" is preferred. If the addresser is not sure whether the letter will be received by a man or a woman, the greeting may be "Ladies and Gentlemen". The salutation should be followed by a colon or a comma.

The salutation is set out flush left and two lines below the inside name and address.

(5) Body of the Letter 正文

The body of the letter is the most important part in a letter. It expresses the addresser's idea, opinion, purpose, etc.. Normally a letter includes three parts: the introductory paragraph, the supporting paragraph and the closing paragraph. The introductory paragraph refers to any previous correspondence or introduces the purpose of the writing. The supporting paragraph provides detailed information. The closing paragraph is short and serves as a request or suggestion.

The body usually begins one or two lines below the salutation. Lines within a paragraph should be single-spaced and double-spaced between paragraphs.

(6) Complimentary Close 客套性结尾

Complimentary close, like salutation, is merely a matter of courtesy and a polite way of ending a letter. It usually consists of a few conventional words or phrases. The first letter of the first word in the close should be capitalized and there is sometimes a comma after the last word. For example:

Yours faithfully,

Faithfully yours,

Yours truly,

Truly yours,

The complimentary close is placed under the body of the letter.

(7) Signature 签名

Every business letter must be signed. The person taking legal responsibility for it should sign a letter in ink. As hand-written signatures are illegible, the name of the signer should be typed below the signature and followed by his job title or position. For example:

John Smith——handwriting signature

John Smith——typewritten signature

President——position

2. Optional Parts 可选部分

The optional parts can be included in a business letter according to the specific situation.

(1) Reference Number 存档编号

The reference number is used to indicate the file number of the addresser's letter or the addressee's letter. When a reference number in a letter is mentioned, the addresser or the addressee will understand immediately which letter is referred to.

If the addresser uses a reference number indicated in the previous letter, the addressee should quote this number after the notation "Your ref." in the reply letter. For example:

Your ref: NMB 129
Our ref: WFR 328

Reference number is typed immediately below the letterhead. If desired, the reference number may form part of the first paragraph of the reply letter. For example:

Dear Sir,
Thank you for your letter, reference No. NMB129, of Sep. 3rd.

Reference number is normally typed three to six lines below the heading.

(2) Attention Line 注意事项线

If the addresser of the letter wishes to direct the letter to a specific person or department, the attention line (abbreviated to Attn.) is used to ensure the letter can reach the right person or department on time. It generally follows the inside name and is typed about two lines above the salutation, underlined and centered. For example:

The Sales Manager
The International Corporation

23 Street, London
U. K.

For the attention of Mr. James Smith or
Attention: Mr. James Smith

(3) Subject 主题

The subject is the general idea of a letter. The subject is especially useful if two companies have a lot of correspondence with each other on a variety of subjects, as it immediately tells the addressee what the letter is about. The subject can refer to invoice number or an L/C number. For example:

Subject: L/C No. 125 for Air Conditioners

As the subject's content and placement indicate its function, the word "subject" can be omitted but underlined. For example:

L/C No. 125 for Air Conditioners

The subject is inserted between the salutation and the body of a letter, usually two lines below the salutation.

(4) Identification Marks 经办人代码

The identification marks are usually the initials of the person who dictated the letter and the initials of the secretary or typists. The former indicates who should shoulder the responsibility of the letter if any dispute concerning the letter occurs. If the dictator and the typist are the same person, this part can be omitted. For example:

LMN/ py
LMN: py

LMN * py

Identification marks may be added below the signature and is usually placed at the left margin.

(5) Enclosure 附件

When something (such as a catalogue, a price list, a sample) is sent together with a letter, the addresser should add the enclosure notation such as "Enclosure" "Encl.", or "Enc.". If more than one enclosure is sent, the addresser had better list the number. For example:

Enclosures (3): 1 Packing List
1 Invoice
1 Letter of Credit

Encl.

Encl. A/S

Enclosure is usually placed at least two lines below identification marks.

(6) Carbon Copy Notation 抄送

If the addresser wants to send a copy of the letter to a third person, indicate with "C. C.", "c. c.", "B. C." (blind copy), or "P. C." (photocopy). If the copies are sent to more than one person, list their names in alphabetical order by surname. For example:

C. C. Mr. Douglas Alien
Mr. Black Ruth

Carbon copy notation is usually placed below the enclosure notation.

(7) Postscript 另启

If the addresser wishes to add something he forgot to mention in the letter or for emphasis, he may add the postscript (abbreviated to PS). In business letters, postscript is not commonly used. This part had better be avoided as far as possible, as it implies that the addresser is careless. So this notation is usually used in the informal styles of letters. Sometimes it serves the purposes as a message that requires emphasis. For example:

P. S.: The sample will reach you in two days.

The postscript can be placed two lines below the carbon copy notation.

Formats of a Business Letter
商务书信的格式

There are various styles of the business English letter. Choice of letter format is a matter of individual taste, but it is better to follow the established practices. The following styles are the most commonly used nowadays.

1. Block Format 平头式,完全齐头式

In the block format, every part of a letter begins from the left margin. As this format is simple and can save the addresser's time, it becomes the most popular format now. However, this format appears unclear to some extent. This disadvantage may be avoided by enlarging the space between the parts. The specific layout of letter in this format is as follows:

Wanli Batteries Group Ltd.
No. 11 Zonghan Industrial Park, Cixi
Zhejiang Province, 315300, P. R. China
Tel: 0574-66540000　　Fax: 0574-66540000 — *Letterhead*

March 3, 2025 ——————— *Date*

Bourdon de France
39, Rue Croix-des-Petits-Champs ——— *Inside Name and Address*
Paris Cedex 01

Dear Mr. Bourdon, ——— *Salutation*

I regret to inform you that an unfortunate error in our quotation No. D 8765 of January 23, 2025 has just come to light. The correct charge for laboratory animal care products and accessories should be US $ 98.95 per set, not $ 89.95 as first quoted.

The mistake is due to a typing error and we are sorry it was not noticed before we sent the document to you last week. — *Body*

We are therefore enclosing an updated quotation sheet for the correction.

Yours sincerely, ——— *Complimentary Close*

Kong Fei
Director of Export ——— *Signature*
Encl. ——— *Enclosure*

2. Indented Format 缩行式

In the indented format, the letterhead is typed in the up-middle part. The date line is placed on the right margin of the paper. Each line in the inside address is indented 2 to 3 spaces. The first line of each paragraph is indented 4 spaces. The complimentary close and the signature are aligned block with the date. The specific layout of letter in this format is as follows:

Wanli Batteries Group Ltd.
No. 11 Zonghan Industrial Park, Cixi
Zhejiang Province, 315300, P. R. China ——— *Letterhead*
Tel: 0574-66540000 Fax: 0574-66540000

March 3, 2025 ——— *Date*

Bourdon de France
39, Rue Croix-des-Petits-Champs ——*Inside Name and Address*
Paris Cedex 01

Dear Mr. Bourdon, ——*Salutation*

I regret to inform you that an unfortunate error in our quotation No. D8765 of January 23, 2025 has just come to light. The correct charge for laboratory animal care products and accessories should be US $ 98.95 per set, not $ 89.95 as first quoted.

The mistake is due to a typing error and we are sorry it was not noticed before we sent the document to you last week. —— *Body*

We are therefore enclosing an updated quotation sheet for the correction.

Yours sincerely, ——*Complimentary close*

Kong Fei
Director of Export ——*Signature*

Encl. ——*Enclosure*

3. Semi-block Format 改良式

Semi-block format is somewhat like block format. All parts begin at the left margin, except the date, complimentary closing and signature which are set against the right-hand margin. It is also named as modified block format. The specific layout of letter in this format is as follows:

Wanli Batteries Group Ltd.
No. 11 Zonghan Industrial Park, Cixi
Zhejiang Province, 315300, P. R. China ——*Letterhead*
Tel: 0574-66540000 Fax: 0574-66540000

March 3, 2025 —— *Date*

Bourdon de France
39, Rue Croix-des-Petits-Champs
Paris Cedex 01
—— *Inside Name and Address*

Dear Mr. Bourdon, —— *Salutation*

I regret to inform you that an unfortunate error in our quotation No. D 8765 of January 23, 2025 has just come to light. The correct charge for laboratory animal care products and accessories should be US $ 98.95 per set, not $ 89.95 as first quoted.

The mistake is due to a typing error and we are sorry it was not noticed before we sent the document to you last week.

We are therefore enclosing an updated quotation sheet for the correction.
— *Body*

Yours sincerely, —— *Complimentary Close*

Kong Fei
Director of Export
—— *Signature*

Encl. —— *Enclosure*

Layout of Envelope for Business Letter
商务书信信封的格式

To ensure the letter can reach the right address and person, the envelope should be written clearly and correctly.

Usually the addresser's name and address is positioned in the upper-left hand corner of the envelope, while the addressee's name and address should be typed about half way down the envelope.

Remember that the addressee's name and address should be identical to the inside name and address in the letter with the name of the addressee on the first line, the house number or road name on the second line, the name of the city, the name of the county and the zip code on the third line and the name of the country on the last line. Most companies have the return address in the upper-left corner of the envelope, giving the same information as the letterhead.

The stamp is put at the upper right corner of the envelope.

Postal directions such as "Registered" "Express" "Confidential" "Private" or "Urgent" should be placed at the bottom left-hand corner. Postal direction such as "Printed Matter" "Sample of No Value" "With Complimentary" "Commercial Paper" should be placed between the return address and the addressee's name and address.

The format of the address on the envelope can be in block or indented style, but it is better to keep the same format as the inside address of the letter.

1. Indented Style 缩行式

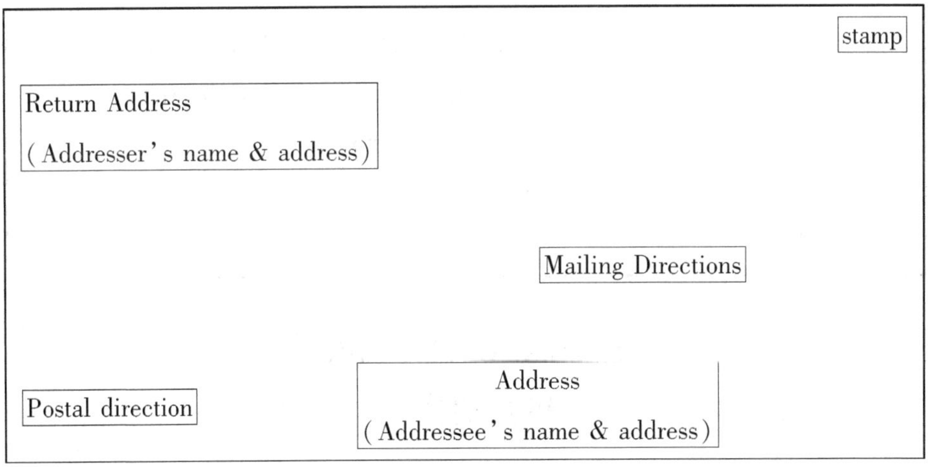

Stamp

General Trading Co.
 234, Main Street
  London, E. C. 1
   England, U. K.

Shanghai Textiles Imp. & Exp. Corp.
 100, Siping Rd. , Hongkou District
  Shanghai, 200080
   P. R. C.

By Airmail

2. Block Style 平头式

Stamp

General Trading Co.
234, Main Street
London, E. C. 1
England, U. K.

Shanghai Textiles Imp. & Exp. Corp.
100, Siping Rd. , Hongkou District
Shanghai, 200080
P. R. C.

By Airmail

Format of Facsimile
传真的格式

The format used for faxes varies considerably, for example, in letter or note form. Fax has its own format and norms.

Fax

FRONTLINE INTERNATIONAL	
TEL: (010)85660000 FAX: (010)85660000	
To:	Fax:
Attn:	Pagc (including this pagc):
From:	Date:
Subject:	Ref No. :

Many companies have their own printed fax form where the company logo, or at least the company name, is in large print. Normally a fax covers the following essential parts.

1. Head Segment 信头

Head segment of a fax consists of the name, address and other contact information of the sender's company such as telephone number, fax number and website.

2. Receiver's Information Block 收件人栏

Receiver's information block gives the information about the addressee's name, title and fax number.

3. Sender's Information Block 发件人栏

Sender's information block gives the information about the sender's name and title.

4. Date 日期

Date should be expressed the same as that in a business letter.

5. Number of Pages 页码数

Number of pages indicates how many pages are included. The number of pages is usually indicated as "1/1" for only one page, "1/2" for the first page of two in total, "2/2" for the second page of two in total.

6. Subject Line 主题

Subject line indicates the major contents of the fax message the same as that in a business letter.

7. Message 正文

Message is the most important part of a fax similar to the body in a business letter. "Best regard" "Best wishes" can be used as complimentary close for the addressee known well to the sender, otherwise, "Sincerely yours" should be used.

In a fax, the sender may use simple language such as short and familiar words to make the message clear. Although faxes could be longer to cover several pages, wordiness should be avoided. The style of a fax message may be formal, informal or neutral depending on the subject and the relationship between the sender and the recipient.

For example:

Fax

Foreign Economic Relations & Trade Committee of What City	
TEL: (010)85660000 FAX: (010)85660000	
To: Consultant for China Swiss Organization for Facilitating Investments	Fax: +41-1-24930000
Attn: Ms Jaana Pekkala	Page (including this page): 2
From: Qiming Di, Commercial Assistant	Date: July 3rd, 2025
Subject: Investment Opportunity	Ref No. :FERTC489

Dear Ms Jaana Pekkala,

We understand from The Swiss Business Guide for China that your organization is helping Swiss firms in seeking opportunities of investing in China and business cooperating with Chinese partners. To establish business relations with your organization and attract Swiss companies' investment here in What, we write to introduce our city, the city of What, as one of the open cities in Liaoning Province, China and also ourselves, Foreign Economic Relations & Trade Committee of What, as a What government initiative to facilitate business relationship with foreign companies.

Our committee provides advice and assistance to What firms seeking to export their services, goods to foreign areas and import goods and services abroad. We also assist What firms in establishment of joint ventures and carry the procedures for examination and approval of joint ventures and foreign sole investment firms. Our Committee can provide What companies with information on the world market and specific commercial opportunities as well as organize trade missions, seminars and business briefings.

Our committee facilitates and encourages investment from other countries into targeted sectors of What economy and maintains active promotion of What through its network of contacts in domestic and abroad areas.

Nowadays, we are seeking foreign investment in the field of capital construction, such as improving of tap water system and highway construction. Also, we are setting up a tannery zone in Tong'erpu, the largest leather clothes producing and wholesaling base in North China. We invite Swiss companies with most favorable polices to set up their firms in any form on tanning, leather processing and sewage treatment.

Any information on investment projects into What and on business cooperation with firms in What is highly appreciated and will be passed on to anyone who have approached us with interest in similar project. You are also invited to our city for investigation and business tour.

Should you have any questions, please feel free to contact us.

Thank you for your attention and looking forward to your prompt reply.

Sincerely yours,

Qiming Di

Commercial Assistant

For Foreign Economic Relations & Trade Committee of What City

Format of E-mail
电子邮件的格式

E-mail is correspondence sent or received on the web. E-mail has its own format and norms.

The format of e-mail is automatically created by the e-mail system itself. It mainly covers the following parts: sender's e-mail address, receiver's e-mail address, subject line, attachment, Cc, message.

To:
From:
Date:
Subject:
Cc:
Attached:

Subject lines in e-mails are similar to those in business letters. The addressee can identify the important e-mails and deal with them promptly with the help of the subject line. Subject lines in e-mails should be specific and concise. When the e-mail message is replied to, the e-mail system automatically creates a subject line "Re: (subject line of the incoming e-mail)." If the subject line is appropriate, it is acceptable. Otherwise, a new subject line should be created. For several rounds of replying to e-mails, "Re: Re: Re" at the start of subject should be avoided. That is, when one is replying to a message but the subject should be changed, change the subject line too.

Cc is the same as that in a business letter. Other addressees' e-mail address should be listed in this blank. It helps the addressee know whom copies of the message are being sent to at the same time.

Attachment in e-mail is the special part to which necessary documents can be attached. If attachment is used, mention it in the message.

Message is the major part of an e-mail. The content and the layout are much similar to those in a business letter. However, an e-mail begins with the salutation and the detailed information about the writer and the company he or she represents will be displayed at the bottom of the e-mail. "Best regard" "Best wishes" can be used as complimentary close for the addressee known well to the sender, otherwise, "Sincerely yours" should be used.

In sending an e-mail, use simple language such as short and familiar words to make the message clear and concise. Adopt polite expressions to create a good image of the sender and the organization he or she represents, though e-mail is the less formal communication channel. Don't cover private information in an e-mail as it guarantees little privacy.

For example:

To: ABC@163.com

From: webadmin9@fastertechnology.com

Date: 21-04-2025, 13:32

Subject: Faster Technology

Cc:

Attached:

Hi Zhou,

Thank you for your application to become a member of Faster Technology. Everyone is welcome to browse around our website but you will need to confirm your membership to have unrestricted access to all areas. To confirm your membership please click on this link:

<http://www.fastertechnology.com/registration.html?tx_srfeuserregister_pi1%5BregHash%5D=47b19d99242d61c2deca>

Or copy and paste it into your browser.

If, for any reason, you do not wish to continue the registration process, or you have received this message in error, please click on this link:

<http://www.fastertechnology.com/registration.html?tx_srfeuserregister_pi1%5BregHash%5D=6562a0d33f2b6adadf81>

Or copy and paste it into your browser.

Please forgive us for any inconvenience we may have caused you.

We would like to welcome you at Faster Technology:

<http://www.fastertechnology.com/>

webadmin9@fastertechnology.com

Notes 注释

1. Formats of a Business Letter 商务书信的格式

商务信函有不同的格式,选用什么样的格式因人而异。常见的格式有以下三种。

(1)Block Format 平头式或齐头式

在平头式商务信函中,所有各部分都是从左边界开始,整封信中均无行首缩格。这种格式简单,易于打印,是商务信函中最常用的格式。

(2)Indented Format 缩行式

在缩行式商务信函中,信件正文每段开始的一行通常都要缩进4~5个空格,其他部分除封内地址外,包括信头、日期、结尾客套语、签名都居中靠右打印。这是一种保守的格式。

(3)Semi-block Format 改良式

在改良式商务信函中,日期、结尾客套语和签名是从纸张中线偏右处开始打印的,其余部分均是从左边界开始打印。这是一种比较保守的格式。

2. Formats of an Envelope 信封的格式

信封的书写格式并没有一定的标准格式,但商务信函中常用的信封格式有缩进式和齐头式两种,与信函格式类似。某些情况下,收信人的姓名、地址等信息出现在信封正面,写信人的相关信息出现在信封背面。

Exercises 练习

Ⅰ. Arrange the following parts of a letter in the correct order and form, either in block format or in indented format.

(1) addresser's name: State Insurance Corporation

(2) addresser's address: 345 Hightower Boulevard, Prince Town, US 12345

(3) addresser's telephone: 03-34570000

(4) addresser's fax: 03-34570000

(5) addressee's address: 25 Silverthorn Garden, BATH Somerset, BA2 9AN, Britain

(6) addressee's name: Mr. R. Jameson

(7) Salutation: Dear Mr. Jameson

(8) Complimentary close: Yours sincerely

(9) Reference initial: DP/MJ

(10) Body of the letter: We should be grateful for these copies of your current catalogues. We are particularly interested in filing cabinets.

(11) Date: May 4th, 2025

(12) Enclosure: 1 pricelist

(13) Signature: David Peters, Sales Manager

(14) Carbon copy notation: Mr. Paul Johnson

(15) Attention line: Business Manager

(16) Subject line: Filling System Catalogues

(17) Rcfcrcncc number: Our ref: SIC 342

Ⅱ. Address an envelope for the above letter, either in block form or in indented form.

Tips

Introduction of Business Writing

Business writing is conventionalized and standardized. Besides efficient and effective messages, you need to give care and attention to the choice of medium, conventions on the presentation of messages, and other professional skills.

With the availability of more options for delivering messages, students need to be aware of the appropriateness of their choice of medium. Letters are seen to be formal, and e-mails informal, with faxes somewhere in between. First contacts are usually made through more formal postal letters or faxes, whereas e-mails are used for follow-up contacts. There are also exceptions. In some countries (e. g. the USA,

Finland), e-mails have assumed almost all the tasks of business letters and made postal letters secondary, if not irrelevant. When you receive an e-mail as the first contact, feel free to e-mail back instead of switching to a letter reply just to be formal. It is worth mentioning here that faxes remain the prominent medium for Chinese business practitioners to contact overseas counterparts, and larger Chinese companies still prefer faxes to e-mails. Besides the business relationship, new or old, and cultural preferences, the choice of medium has other underlying reasons. These can be time pressures, convenience and communicative purpose. Under pressure of time, faxes and e-mails can be the right choices. Furthermore, faxes are more convenient and flexible than e-mails. Any sheet of A4 paper can be put through a fax machine and no special hardware or software is required to prepare a document which includes graphs, photographs or diagrams. With regard to communicative purpose, postal letters are appropriate for confidential messages, whereas faxes and e-mails are suitable for ordinary messages, such as making requests and supplying information.

Whatever medium of delivery your message goes through, your aim should be to ensure a high standard in all important areas: layout, medium-related protocols and structural frames, grammar, spelling, and punctuation. Attention and care given to these details will help create and enhance goodwill towards yourself and the company you represent. Poor letters, faxes and e-mails can destroy the very confidence and goodwill they seek to establish and maintain.

Guide to Writing

Letters, faxes and e-mails are among the dominant means of business correspondence. A fax can be used as we use an envelope and mail service. It can be seen either as just another way of sending messages or as a message type of its own. Its advantage over a letter is speed. The e-mail has also developed its own "netiquette", being a message type of its own, and has the following guidelines:

1. An e-mail is informal, and less suitable for confidential messages. Thus, ask yourself: is an e-mail the right method for communicating this particular message?

2. Compose offline.

3. Key in the right e-mail address.

4. Avoid misleading subject lines.

5. Use the inverted pyramid approach in organizing all the necessary information.

6. Keep sentences and paragraphs short because it is easier to read them on the computer screen.

7. Avoid using CAPITALS, because some people take it as "shouting" and consider it rude. Instead, type the message in capital and small letters for easy reading.

8. Care about correctness. Check grammar, spellings and punctuations.

9. Avoid letter combinations and emotions in business correspondence. Examples are ASAP (as soon as possible), FYI (for your information), CU (see you).

10. Announce attachments. If you are sending a lengthy attachment, tell your addressee about it.

Chapter 2 Writing Principles of Business Letters
商务书信的写作原则

Learning Objectives

- Comprehend the writing principles of the business letter
- Comprehend the effective construction of paragraphs
- Master the effective beginnings and endings of the business letter

学习目标：了解商务书信的写信原则、段落结构，掌握商务书信中有效的开头与结尾方式。

Introduction

The major objectives of business correspondence are to convey a message and obtain complete understanding between the writer and the addressee. The writer must make sure that the letter should be free from the slightest possibility of being misunderstood. There are certain essential qualities of business letters, which can be expressed in the following "7 Cs" principles.

Principles of Good Communication
良好沟通的原则

1. Clarity 清楚

Clarity is the first requirement of an effective letter. The addresser should try his/her best to express his/her idea clearly to enable the addressee to understand it.

For this purpose, the addresser should keep in mind the purpose of writing the letter and use appropriate words in correct sentence structures to convey his or her meaning. So the addresser should avoid ambiguous expressions. Otherwise the addressee may misunderstand the letter. To make the message clear, the addresser must express it in well-constructed sentences and paragraphs. Compare:

As to the steamers sailing from Shanghai to San Francisco, we have bimonthly direct services.

As to the steamers sailing from Shanghai to San Francisco, we have two direct sailings every month.

As to the steamers sailing from Shanghai to San Francisco, we have a direct sailing every two months.

We sent you 5 samples yesterday of the goods which you requested in your letter of May 5 by air.

We sent you yesterday, by air, 5 samples of the goods which you requested in your letter of May 5.

My suggestions are similar to your proposals that were put forward a week ago.

My suggestions that were put forward a week ago are similar to your proposals.

A telex was sent by us yesterday.

We sent you a telex yesterday.

Sometimes the parallel structure can promote clarity. For example:

They refused not only to make payment but also to return the goods.

There is also a saving in freight charges when separate consignments intended for the same port of destination are carried in one container and an additional saving on insurance, because of the lower premiums charged for container shipped goods.

2. Courtesy 礼貌

Courtesy is not mere politeness. The addresser should try to understand and respect the addressee's opinions. It is not necessary to stress the importance of courtesy in the letter. Normally, when talking about courtesy, keep in mind You-attitude. That means the addresser should make addressee the focus of the letter, for example, by putting himself in the addressee's place. This "You-attitude" is very useful in contacting the customers.

When the addressee receives a letter, he or she should try his or her best to reply the letter promptly, as any delay in replying shows lack of courtesy. If the addresser is not able to accept the request made in the incoming letter immediately, he or she had better inform the addressee of the reason and let the addressee know when he or she can accept the request. Even if one receives a rude and unreasonable letter, he should reply with understanding and courtesy. Compare:

We cannot comply with your request.

We are afraid we cannot comply with your request.

We will give you a 3% discount for this new order.

As our new client, you will enjoy a 3% discount.

You have failed to establish the L/C covering your order No. 234 in time.

The L/C covering your order No. 234 hasn't reached us. Please check it with your bank.

3. Conciseness 简洁

Conciseness means expressing the opinions in the fewest possible words. In other words, a concise business letter should be short and to the point. The omission of wordy jargon can help to make a letter clearer and at the same time more concise. A concise business letter should express briefly but it shouldn't be achieved with the sacrifice of completeness, clarity or courtesy. Compare:

In compliance with your request, we will send you the sample next week.

At your request, we will send you the sample next week.

Re your letter of 21st inst., in connection with our account, we are remitting our check herewith, as per your request, in the amount of $100.00.

As requested in your letter of 21 June, we are enclosing our check for $100.00.

We require furniture which is of the new type.

We require new-type furniture.

4. Concreteness 具体

Concreteness means making the message specific, definite and vivid. The addresser must ensure that the letter contain all the information the addressee needs. According to the commercial practices, the addresser should state in the offer the detailed contents, such as the specific shipping date, description of the goods, quantity; otherwise it will be hard for the addressee to decide whether to accept the offer or not. Compare:

Please ship the goods as soon as possible.

Please ship the goods before September 4, 2025 by direct sailing.

As requested in your recent letter, we have already sent the samples to you.

As requested in your letter dated December 3, we sent you the samples by air on December 13.

These brakes can stop a car within a short distance.

These Goodson power brakes can stop a two-ton car within 24 feet.

5. Consideration 体贴

Consideration means that the addresser should be considerate of the addressee in order to maximize mutual understanding. To be successful in transmitting the message, the addresser must evaluate the addressee's situation and then write the letter. Consideration emphasizes You-attitude rather than We-attitude. When writing a letter, keep the addressee's request, needs, desires as well as his feelings in mind. Compare:

We are shipping your order of September 24 this afternoon.

2,000 sets of Air Conditioners you ordered will be shipped this afternoon and should reach you by September 29.

I am quite sure that this is exactly what is needed.

I am quite sure that this is exactly what you need.

To help us improve our production schedule, we must ask you to place orders two months in advance.

If you place orders two months in advance, it will help us improve our production schedule.

6. Correctness 正确

Correctness means providing accurate facts and figures and avoiding the mistakes in relation to spelling, grammar and punctuation. Special attention should be paid to correctness in business letters as detailed information regarding the dates, specifications, prices and quantities will be stated. However a minor mistake may lead to disputes between the concerned parties. Compare:

We hardly imported any food last month.

We imported hardly any food last month.

The price of our product is $ 100 per metric ton CIF Singapore.

The price of our product is US $ 100 per metric ton CIF Singapore.

Please contact with our Sales Department if you would like to act as our agent in your country.

Please contact our Sales Department if you would like to act as our agent in your country.

7. Completeness 完整

Like any other letters, a proper business letter should be complete. Completeness means all the necessary information should be covered. Incomplete information will fail to enable the business person to seize the business opportunities of doing mutually beneficial trade.

Construction of the Body of a Business Letter 商务书信正文的结构

The body of a letter normally includes the beginning, the topic and the ending. Effective construction helps make the messages stand out.

A paragraph consists of several sentences closely related to each other. Normally the sentences deal with the same subject matter. Paragraph is very important to effective communication besides 7 "Cs". How to design paragraphs is hard to explain, which depends on the desires of writing. Sometimes a paragraph may consist of a single sentence. The following methods may help organize the paragraph in an effective way.

1. Focus on One Topic or Idea 集中至一个主题或想法

Everything in a paragraph should focus on one topic or idea. For example:

The trade terms refer to using a brief English concept or abbreviation to indicate the formation of the unit price and determine the responsibilities, expenses and risks borne by two parties.

When the two parties determine to adopt certain trade terms, all other clauses in the contract shall be in conformity with them. Therefore, in international trade, we usually make use of certain trade terms to define the nature of the contract, such as FOB contract or CIF contract, to determine expenses and risks as well as their rights and obligations accordingly.

In the first paragraph, it defines the phrase "the trade terms". In the second paragraph, it centers on the relationship between trade terms and the nature of the contract.

2. Make the Paragraph in Order 有序安排段落

Sentences in a paragraph should be placed in logical order, which means that the preceding sentence should lead naturally to the next one. For example:

Value added tax, always shortened as VAT, is a tax on exchange of goods and/or service. It is levied on the added value that results from each exchange. It differs from a sales tax because a sales tax is levied on the total value of the exchange. For this reason, a VAT is neutral with respect to the number of passages that there are between the producer and the final consumer. A VAT is an indirect tax, in that the tax is collected from someone other than the person who actually bears the cost of the tax (namely the seller rather than the consumer). To avoid double taxation on final consumption, exports are usually not subject to VAT and VAT charged under such circumstances is usually refundable.

In this paragraph, the first two sentences define the phrase "value added tax". The next two sentences introduce the difference between VAT and a sales tax. The other sentences indicate the nature of VAT.

If the first sentence states the topic of the paragraph, the following sentences should support it and amplify it. To achieve this, the addresser must plan thoroughly what he wishes to say and then arrange the idea into the most suitable order.

Effective Beginnings
有效的开头

The opening sentence or paragraph is very important as it makes the first impression on the addressee. The effective opening is the key to the success of a business letter.

1. Introductory Opening 介绍性开头

To attract the addressee, it is proper to indicate in the first sentence the reason for the addresser to write the letter and his objectives. For example:

We have seen your advertisement in China Daily concerning the new fabrics available at present and we should be obliged if you would send us your pattern books for the complete range of these fabrics together with your price list.

2. Natural Opening 自然式开头

Normally, when a addressee receives a letter, he should reply to it. The first sentence in his reply may refer to the previous letter. He should not only indicate the date of the correspondence but also the main contents in it, such as the addresser's interest in certain products or his desire to obtain a catalogue, etc. For example:

In reply to your fax of June 3 in which you asked us to make an offer for our Blanket (Catalogue No. 22), we wish to confirm our fax dispatched on June 6 for an offer without engagement as follows...

Effective Endings
有效的结尾

The closing sentence or paragraph is frequently used to sum up a letter or to emphasis the requests the addresser wishes the addressee to respond to.

1. Specific Ending 具体性的结尾

In the ending, the addresser expresses his desire specifically. That means the addresser will not use timeworn expressions. For example:

All these items are urgently required by our customers. We, therefore, hope you will make delivery at an early date.

We are looking forward to receiving your shipping advice as soon as possible.

2. Conclusive Ending 总结性的结尾

If a letter is long and complex, the addresser may summarize the main contents in the last sentence or in the last paragraph. For example:

In view of the above, you are requested to increase the amount of your L/C by US $ 150, making a total of US $ 2,638, and also to extend the time of shipment to 21st December. Your prompt attention to this matter will be appreciated.

Exercises 练习

Ⅰ. Improve the following sentences.

1. We have already received your L/C, for which please accept our thanks.
2. Allow us to state that we sincerely hope you will give your careful

consideration to our proposals.

3. I am pleased to tell you a piece of good news. After 20 years of service you are rewarded by being appointed the managing director. Congratulations!

4. Please don't hesitate to get in touch with us in case you have any questions.

5. Referring to your communication of recent date, we hereby make you an offer as follows.

6. Effectuation of a decision will have to be delayed by me until next month.

7. We decide in Melbourne last spring to continue the talks at this Fair.

8. He needs someone to help him promote sales badly.

9. We must deny your request for sole agency.

10. Demonstration of the new machines can be arranged for those interested.

11. If this change is desired, it would be necessary that the attached form be signed and dated.

12. This drawing is enclosing for your approval.

13. In all probability, we are likely to suffer a loss this quarter.

14. It is your turn to make an acquisition of compensation.

15. In view of you are our old customer, we prepare to give you a discount of 5%.

Ⅱ. Choose the best opening or closing.

1. a. We received your letter of May 7. Here is a copy of our price list you asked for.
   b. Here is our price list you asked for in your letter of May 7.
   c. We enclose herewith a copy of our price list for which you asked.
2. a. We are writing to answer your questions.
   b. We sent you this morning our latest catalogue you requested in your letter of yesterday.
   c. We beg to state that your letter of October 3 has been given careful consideration.
3. a. Hoping to be able to keep in touch with you for the years to come, we

remain.

b. We hope to have frequent contacts with you.

c. Hoping to be in frequent contact with you and assuring you of our best attention.

4. a. Please be assured of our best attention.

b. Thank you again.

c. Once again, may we express our appreciation to you.

Ⅲ. Organize the following sentences into a sensible order or a natural method.

1. Is there any way in which you can assist us with finance? Our hire purchase customers tend to spread payments over 2 or 3 years. Our expansion is being held up at present by a lack of finance. What would be the terms and arrangements if we ask you to assist us? We are an expanding electronic supply store selling to retailers and also to ordinary customers on hire purchase terms.

2. We are glad to say that we have found a ship which we think will serve you very well. The ship is now at Antwerp and can be ready to load at four or five days definite notice. We thank you for your enquiry of May 9. The ship is m. v. Carnilia with a cargo capacity of about 5,000 registered tons. And for a charter of 12 months the owners are prepared to consider a special rate. We will prepare the charter party and send it to you as soon as we receive your cable confirmation.

3. The store received your credit application form on time, but it was filled out incorrectly. As the form indicates, your signature should be written on the bottom of both pages, but you neglected to do this. Your form is being returned to you for proper signing.

Tips

Barriers to Communication

An analysis of barriers to communication will help people communicate in more effective and efficient ways.

DIFFERENCE IN PERCEPTION is one of the barriers that may cause ineffective communication. Individuals of different ages, cultural backgrounds, and national origins often have different perception of what being discussed. They usually use their learning, culture, and experiences to interpret what they are told.

LACK OF INTEREST in the subject matter, on the part of a speaker or a listener, a addresser or a reader, can be serious deterrent to the reception of ideas. A reader or a listener who does not see the benefit from what he is expected to do usually ignores or even goes against the idea he receives. Being not interested in the topic concerned, he is often found difficult to motivate or to cooperate with the initiator.

DIFFERENCE IN LANGUAGE is probably a more common barrier to communication. People speak hundreds of languages in the world. They use their own language (different words, sentences, idioms, and sounds) to convey ideas, facts, and feelings. Even when communicating in a common language, people sometimes found it difficult to interpret a statement in the same way because some semantic problems may arise in the understanding of the same message.

CULTURAL DIFFERENCES strike people the most obviously in another culture. Culture is what people grow up in. Beginning in childhood, he or she learns the behaviors, habits, and attitudes that are acceptable to those around. Under the surface all human beings are alike members of the family of man. This belief causes people to expect that their own cultures are natural, appropriate, and acceptable to others. However, this is not true in practice. Views on the following factors may differ greatly from culture to culture:

Language—spoken, written, verbal, nonverbal, native, or foreign;

Attitudes and Values—toward man, nature, time, change, materialism, and others;

Religion—rituals, sacred objects, and beliefs;

Law—civil, or business;

Associations—family, class, group, institution, nation, or society.

As culture is so complex, and international business activities are sometimes so intricate, it is sometimes rather difficult to communicate successfully across cultures. However, people can succeed if they learn about the culture before beginning to communicate.

The above examples of barriers to communication are only a few of those that can be cited. Differences in political systems, economic development, export and import policies, and business practices have always created problems.

As a student of international business or a foreign trader, one should be aware that international business communication involves more variables than one might initially expect. The success or failure will very much depend on skills in communicating in a cross-cultural environment. In order to achieve these skills, we can begin by making a serious study of languages, basic theories and practices in international business. Beyond all these, we have to train ourselves for successful intercultural communication.

Writing a Good Letter, Fax or Email

1. Plan ahead. Decide what you want to say before you start writing. Make notes.

2. Look professional. A clean, logical format gives the best impression. A crowded or over-designed page will distract the reader from your message. Leave a line space between paragraphs.

3. Keep it simple. Don't use complicated language. Keep your sentences short—one idea in each sentence. Any sentence longer than two typed lines is probably too long. Shorter sentences are easier to read.

4. Put yourself in your reader's place. Try to imagine how you would respond to the same letter. Have you given the right impression?

5. Be friendly. Your correspondence should read like a conversation with the reader. Use your reader's name if you know it: "Dear Ms. Green". You want her to know that you wrote the letter just for her. Use "I", "we" and "you".

6. Reply in the same style. If someone writes a friendly letter to you using

contractions such as "don't" "can't", use the same style in your reply.

7. Re-read the letter before sending it. Does it give the right impression? Check for spelling mistakes and punctuation errors. Make sure that all the information you give is accurate.

Chapter 3 Establishment of Business Relations

建立业务关系

Learning Objectives

- Know the sources of obtaining information about the potential business partners
- Master the steps in writing letters about establishing business relations

学习目标:了解获知潜在贸易伙伴信息的渠道,掌握建立业务关系信件写作的步骤。

Cases Study

On Dec. 19th, 2025, Sun Liang started to work in Jin Yuan Import & Export Corporation (abbreviated to Jin Yuan Corp.) which was founded in 1998. Jin Yuan Corp. majors in the export of textiles and the exports are well accepted in France, Germany, Italy, Britain, and so on. In addition, Jin Yuan Corp. has already built reliable relations with many domestic suppliers.

On Dec. 21st, 2025, Sun Liang learned on www. alibaba. com that Fashion General Trading Co. (abbreviated to FG) demanded for textiles.

Question: If Jin Yuan Corp. desired to establish business relations with FG, what should Sun Liang do?

Introduction

In international trade, a company must establish business relations with the foreign party as its first step to start or to expand its international business. Therefore, the establishment of business relations is of vital importance to any company, an old-established company or a newly-established one.

If a company wishes to expand a new foreign market to sell its products or purchase some commodities, it should seek its prospective trade partners. Usually it can secure the necessary information about the potential trade partner through the following channels: the introduction from its subsidiary branches or agents abroad; the recommendation from its business connections at home and abroad; the advertisements or information from the publications, such as television, broadcasting, newspaper, magazines; internet; the banks; Chambers of Commerce at home and abroad; Commercial Counselor's Offices at home and abroad; market survey; trade delegations and groups visiting abroad; self-introduction or enquiries from the merchants abroad; attendance at trade fairs and exhibitions held both at home and abroad.

Having obtained the desired name and address of a foreign company from one of the above sources, the company can write a letter to express its desire to establish business relations with the prospective trade partner. Such letters usually include the following contents:

(1) Indicate the source of the information about the addressee, i. e. where or from whom the addresser obtains the addressee's name and address;

(2) Indicate its desire to establish business relations with the addressee, if possible, stating the commodities it desires to sell or purchase;

(3) Make a self-introduction, such as its business scope, its history, etc;

(4) State the reference about its financial standing if possible;

(5) Express its expectation of cooperation and an early reply from the addressee. If the addresser is an importer, he may make an enquiry for catalogues, samples, price lists, etc.

When introducing the information on the business scope of the addresser's company, the addresser should make it brief, clear, concise and focus on the information most attractive and important to the addressee.

After the addressee receives such a letter, he should answer it without any delay and with courtesy so as to create goodwill and leave a good impression on the reader.

Specimen Letters

样信

Letter 1: Letter from Jin Yuan Corp. to FG

JIN YUAN IMPORT AND EXPORT CO., LTD.
NO. 118 XUEYUAN ROAD, BEIJING, CHINA, 100081
Tel: 86-10-87160000 Fax: 86-10-87160000

Dec. 21st, 2025

FASHION GENERAL TRADING CO.
15 RUE MARQUISE DU CHATELET
ZONE INDUSTRIELLE FAIRNCERIES
12500, LUNEVILLE, FRANCE
Tel: 0033-3-82340000
Fax: 0033-3-82340000

Dear Sirs,

We have **obtained** your name and address **from** www. alibaba. com and are glad to learn that you demand for textiles at present.

We have the pleasure of introducing ourselves to you. Our company, Jin Yuan Import & Export Corporation (referred to as "Jin Yuan Corp."), was founded in 1998. At present we **major in** the **export** of textiles and our **exports** are well accepted in France, Germany, Italy, Britain, and so on. In addition, we have built reliable relations with the major domestic suppliers of textiles.

In order to give you a general idea of our products, we are **enclosing** a copy of our latest catalog. We feel sure that we can supply large quantities of textiles on favorable terms if we receive your specific enquires.

We are looking forward to your specific enquiries at an early date.

Yours faithfully,
Lion Li
Sales Manager
Jin Yuan Import & Export Corporation, Ltd.

Enclosure: 1 catalogue

Letter 2: Letter from an Exporter to an Importer

Dear Sirs,

On recommendation of our **Commercial Counselor's Office** in your country, we are glad to learn that you are one of the leading importers of embroideries in your country.

We have pleasure of introducing ourselves to you as **a state corporation majoring in** the **export** of embroideries in China for over 30 years and our products are **well accepted** worldwide. Now we express our desire to **enter into business relations** with you in this **line**.

In order to give you a general idea of our commodities, we are enclosing a copy of our recent **catalogue. Quotations** and samples will be sent to you **upon receipt of** your **specific enquiries**.

We are looking forward to your favorable reply.

Yours faithfully,

Encl.

Letter 3: Letter from an Importer to an Exporter

Dear Sirs,

We have obtained your name and address in the recent issue of *International Trade* and are now writing to you for the **establishment** of business relations between us.

We are very well connected with the major dealers here of silk products. At present, we are very interested in your embroidered silk handkerchief and believe that we can sell large quantities of them if we get your competitive offers. Meanwhile, please let us have all necessary information **concerning** your exports.

As to our **standing**, we refer you to the National City Bank of New York, New York.

Yours faithfully,

Words & Phrases 词汇

1. obtain from... 从……获知

类似的表述有：

We owe your name and address to your Chamber of Commerce which has informed us that you are the largest importer of minerals in your country.

我们从贵方商会得知贵方的名称和地址，并了解到贵方是贵国矿产品最大的进口商。

Having had your name and address from the Commercial Councilor's Office of the Swedish Embassy in Beijing, we now avail ourselves of this opportunity to write to you and see if we can enter into business relations with your company.

我们从瑞典驻北京大使馆商务参赞处得知贵方的名称和地址，现借此机会给贵方写信以建立业务关系。

Through the courtesy of Mr. Wang, we learn that you are one of the leading importers of electric goods in your country and wish to enter into business relations with you.

我们通过王先生了解到贵方是贵国电子产品领先的进口商之一，希望能和贵方建立业务关系。

We are indebted to ABC Co., for your name and address.

我们从 ABC 公司得知贵方的名称和地址。

From (Through) sb., we learn your name and address.

通过××，我们得知贵方的名称和地址。

2. major in 主营

Our company majors in Chinese light industrial products.

我方主营中国轻工产品。

类似的表述有：

We have been told that your corporation specializes in the export of various light industrial products.

我们被告知贵方专门出口各类轻工产品。

Our company handles exclusively watches and clocks of all sorts.

我们专营各类手表和钟表。

3. export n.（单数）出口，（复数）出口货

We handle the export of metals.

我们经营五金的出口。

What are chief exports of Canada?

加拿大主要的出口商品是什么？

与 export 相关的短语：export control 出口管制，amount of exports 出口额，export declaration 出口申报单，export license 出口许可证，export quota 出口配额

v. 出口

We export a large quantity of textiles now.

我们现在大量出口纺织品。

exportation n. 出口（一般可与名词 export 单数通用）

We are engaged in the exportation of Chinese light industrial products.

我们从事中国轻工产品的出口。

exporter n. 出口商

They are leading exporters of electric goods.

它们是电子产品领先的出口商。

4. enclose v. 随函附寄，把（文件等）放入信封内

We are enclosing (herewith) our commercial invoice in duplicate.

我们随附一式两份的商业发票。

Please refer to the price list enclosed in (herewith) our letter of August 5.

请参阅我方 8 月 5 日随信附寄的价目单。

过去分词 enclosed 做表语时，常倒装置于句首。

Enclosed are two copies of our price list.

随附的是两份我方的价目单。

过去分词 enclosed 做宾语补语时，常倒置于句首或置于谓语动词后。

Enclosed please find a copy of our price list.

Please find enclosed a copy of our price list.

请查收我们随附的一份价目单。

过去分词 enclosed 可做名词用，前面加定冠词。

We believe you will find the enclosed interesting.

我们相信你们会认为附件是有趣的。

enclosure n. 附件(用缩写 Encl. 或 Enc.)

We have received your letter of May 5 along with two enclosures.

我们收到贵方 5 月 5 日的来信及两份附件。

5. on the recommendation of 通过……的推荐

On the recommendation of Messrs. Smith & Evans, we have learnt your name and shall be pleased to establish business relations with your firm.

承蒙 Smith 先生和 Evans 先生的推荐,我们得知贵方的名称,并愿意与贵方建立业务关系。

6. recommend v. 推荐,建议

We recommend your acceptance of our offer as the price for this article will be increased soon.

我们建议贵方接受我们的报价,因为该商品的价格不久将上涨。

We request you to recommend them some articles that suit their market.

我们请贵方给他们推荐一些适合他们市场的产品。

We recommend that you contact them directly for their offer.

我方建议贵方直接和他们联系获取报价。

7. Commercial Counselor's Office 商务参赞处

We planned to establish a Commercial Counselor's Office in Libya one year ago.

一年前我们计划在利比亚设立商务参赞处。

8. state corporation 国有企业

state-operated corporation 国营公司, state-owned corporation 国有公司, state-run enterprise 国营企业

We are a wholly state-owned corporation majoring in Chinese silk scarves.

我们是一家主营中国真丝围巾的国有公司。

9. be well accepted 广受好评

Our products are well accepted all over the world.

我们的产品在世界各地广受好评。

类似的表述有:enjoy great popularity, be most popular with, enjoy fast sales, be universally acknowledged

The goods have enjoyed great popularity in the world market.

产品在世界市场上享有盛誉。

The goods are most popular with our customers.

产品非常受我们顾客的欢迎。

The goods have commanded a good market.

The goods are selling fast.

The goods enjoy fast sales.

产品畅销。

The goods are universally acknowledged.

产品被普遍认可。

10. enter into business relations 建立业务关系

类似的表述有：enter into trade relations, enter into trade relationship, establish business relations 与……建立业务关系

We shall be pleased to enter into direct business relations with your company.

我们很高兴能和贵方建立直接的业务关系。

We are writing hoping to enter into business relationship with you.

我们给贵方写信的目的是，希望能和贵方建立业务关系。

11. line n. 行业，领域

表示经营的类似表述有：trade in, deal in, handle, be engaged in

This company has been in the line of light industrial products for thirty years.

该公司在轻工产品领域已经营 30 年。

Their chief line is the import of air conditioners.

他们的主营业务是进口空调。

12. catalogue n. 目录

与 catalogue 相关的短语：classified catalogue 分类目录, descriptive catalogue 带有说明的目录, illustrated catalogue 有插图的目录, catalogue of industrial products 工业产品目录

For most of the articles in the catalogue, we can supply from stock.

对于商品目录中的多数商品，我们可以供现货。

13. quotation n. 行市,报价

make/send/give/cable sb. a quotation for 给某人发/电报某商品的报价

Please make us your lowest quotation for iron nails.

请给我方报贵方铁钉的最低价。

买方提及卖方报价时,用 quotation of。

Your quotation of iron nails is too high to be workable.

贵方铁钉的价格太高了,无法运作。

quote v. 报价,除单价外还包括数量、交货期、付款方式等

quote sb. a price for sth. 给某人报价某商品

Please quote us your lowest price for iron nails.

请给我方报贵方铁钉的最低价。

Please quote us for Iron Nails.

请给我方做一个铁钉的报价。

Please quote your lowest price.

请报最低价。

14. specific inquiries 具体询盘

inquiry n. 调查,询问,询盘,要货

make inquiry 表示询问,很少用单数(指具体商品时通常用介词 for;指一般情况通常用介词 about)

We will make inquiries about the business possibilities of your new products.

我们想询问关于贵方新产品的销售可能性。

We thank you for your enquiry for carpets.

感谢贵方对地毯的询盘。

At the moment there are only small inquiries for this class of goods.

目前,对于这类商品要货很少。

inquire v. 询问,询价,要货

We acknowledge receipt of your letter of May 30 inquiring for alarm clocks.

贵方 5 月 30 日关于闹钟询盘的信件已收悉。

15. upon receipt of/on receipt of 一旦收到,一收到……就……

类似的表述有:on receipt of, after receipt of

We shall load the goods on board upon receipt of your letter of credit.

一收到贵方的信用证,我们就将对货物装船。

Upon receipt of your shipping instruction, we shall make necessary arrangement.

一收到贵方的装运指示,我们将做出必要的安排。

We are in receipt of your letter dated Feb. 28th, from which we have learnt that you hope to enter into trade relations with us.

我们收到了贵方2月28日的来信,从中我们了解到你们希望与我们建立业务关系。

16. concerning prep. 关于

We have not received your letter of credit concerning your Order No. 345.

我们尚未收到有关贵方第345号订单的信用证。

17. standing n. 状况,信誉 a. 固定的,长期的

与 standing 相关的短语有:financial standing/status/position/performance 财务状况,credit and financial standing 资信状况,standing cost 长期成本,standing orders 长期订单

Please inform us of the financial standing of ABC Company.

请告知我们 ABC 公司的财务状况。

As to the financial standing, this company is reliable.

就财务状况而言,该公司是可靠的。

Owing to the long-standing friendly business relations between us, we offer you the most favorable terms.

鉴于你我之间的长期友好关系,我们现给贵方报最优惠的条款。

Useful Sentences 常用句型

1. We have come to know your name and address from the Commercial Counselor's Office of Chinese Embassy in London. We now avail ourselves of this opportunity to establish business relations with you.

我们从中国驻伦敦大使馆商务参赞处得知贵方的名称和地址,借此机会想和你们建立业务关系。

2. We owe your name and address to the Chamber of Commerce in your

country, through whom we learn that you are in the market for silk products.

承蒙贵国商会的介绍,我们得知贵方的名称和地址,并了解到贵方欲购买丝绸产品。

3. We have read your advertisement on the www. alibaba. com and have pleasure in building up business relations with you.

我们看到了你们在 www. alibaba. com 上的广告,很高兴与你们建立业务关系。

4. We take the liberty to introduce ourselves as exporters of silk products, which we have been exporting to Europe and Japan for many years.

冒昧地自我介绍,作为丝绸产品的出口商,我们向欧洲以及日本出口丝绸产品已很多年。

5. We are writing to you in the hope that we can open up business relations with your firm.

我们给你们写信,目的是能与贵公司建立业务关系。

6. In order to extend our export business to your country, we wish to enter into direct business relations with you.

为了扩大在贵国的出口业务,我们希望与贵方建立直接的业务关系。

7. We wish to express our desire to trade with you in silk products.

我们想表达与贵方从事丝绸产品贸易的愿望。

8. As you are one of the leading importers of camera in India, we have pleasure in contacting you in the hope of establishing business relations with you.

贵方是印度领先的照相机进口商之一,我们很高兴与贵方联系并希望与贵方建立业务关系。

9. We wish to introduce ourselves to you as a state-owned corporation dealing exclusively in silk products.

我们愿向贵方做自我介绍,我们是一家专营丝绸产品的国有公司。

10. To give you a general idea of our products, we enclose a complete set of leaflets of various products being handled by our corporation with detailed specifications and methods of packing.

为使贵方对我方产品有一个大致的了解,我们随函附上一套包含详细规格和包装方法在内的完整的有关我公司所经营的各种产品的宣传单。

11. You may be interested to know that for over 20 years we have been engaged in manufacturing electronic machinery of all specifications and exporting them to users all over the world.

贵方也许有兴趣了解,20 多年来,我们一直从事各种规格电子机械的生产并将它们出口至世界各地。

12. To acquaint you with the pharmaceutical and industrial chemicals we handle, we are sending you, under separate cover, several pamphlets for your reference.

为使贵方了解我们所经营的医药和工业化学品,我们将另邮给你们一些宣传册,供贵方参考。

13. Silk products fall/come within the scope of our business activities.

丝绸产品属于我们的业务范围。

14. Our bankers are the Hong Kong & Shanghai Banking Corporation in Hong Kong and they can provide you with the information about our business and finances.

我们的银行是位于香港的香港上海银行股份公司,它们可以为您提供关于我公司业务资信状况的信息。

15. If you require any information about our financial standing, we would refer you to International Commercial Bank of China.

如果贵方需要关于我们财务状况的任何资料,请向中国国际商业银行咨询。

Exercises 练习

Ⅰ. Fill in the blanks with the proper word.

Dear Sirs,

We have____your address____the China Business Directory and are now writing to you for the____of business____.

We are very well____with all the____dealers here of silk products. At present, we are very____in your embroidered silk handkerchief and feel____we can sell large quantities of them if we get your offers____competitive prices.

As____ our standing, we are permitted to ____ the Bank of America, Washington, as a____.

We look____to your early reply.

Yours faithfully,

Ⅱ. Translate the following sentences into Chinese.

1. On the recommendation of ABC Corporation in New York, we have learned with pleasure the name of your firm.

2. We take the opportunity to introduce ourselves as an exporter of ceramic teapots and have experience in this particular line for many years.

3. Specializing in the export of Chinese light industrial products, we express our desire to trade with you in this line.

4. We are willing to enter into business relations with your firm on the basis of equality and mutual benefit.

5. We are in the market for fertilizers.

6. Our market survey informs us that you are interested in the import of machinery.

7. We shall be glad to send quotations and samples upon receipt of your concrete enquiries.

8. Our company is a large foreign trade company engaged in import and export business for nearly 20 years with a very good reputation.

9. Being a large auto repair shop chain in India, we have 52 locations with a strong demand for car parts and maintenance machinery.

10. We are given to understand that you are potential buyers of Chinese silk products, which come within the scope of our business activities.

Ⅲ. Translate the following sentences into English.

1. 作为日本丝绸产品主要进口商之一,我们写信给贵公司,希望与贵公司建立直接贸易关系。

2. 玩具出口属于我们的经营范围。

3. 我们从我国驻法国商务参赞处获悉,贵公司对中国制造的家用电器很感兴趣。

4. 鉴于我方专营轻工产品出口业务,我方愿与贵方在这方面开展贸易。

5. 为使贵方对我方产品有全面的了解,我方将另函寄去一本目录,供贵方参考。

6. 我们利用此机会致函贵方以了解可否与贵方建立贸易关系。
7. 贵方如能告诉我们是否对上述生意感兴趣,我们将深表感谢。
8. 我们有幸自荐,盼望有机会与贵方合作,扩展业务。
9. 我们在业界有良好的关系,对于经营此类产品的进口业务有着丰富的经验。
10. 我们的产品驰名中外,相信在贵国将有很大的市场潜力。

Ⅳ. Translate the following letter into Chinese.

Dear Sirs,

From the e-mail sent back by our Toronto Office, we know that you are one of the firms of good standing and reliability in Toronto and are particularly interested in the export of various papers.

By this letter, we are approaching you with a view to entering into business relations with your company and hope to receive soon your catalogue and other printed matters for reference.

Of recent years, we have done much business with the largest and most prominent company in your district. As is well known to you, the possibilities of importing the foreign products are very great here, especially as we are now developing our economy.

We are confident that we shall be able to give you big orders if you would cooperate with us on delivery, price and quality.

We look forward to establishing friendly relationship with you soon.

Yours faithfully,

Ⅴ. Translate the following letter into English.

敬启者:

我们从我们当地的商会那儿得知贵公司的名称与地址,现写信给贵公司,愿与贵公司建立业务关系。

我们是广州最大的化工品进口商之一,并与这里所有的批发商和零售商关系良好。为此,我们肯定,只要贵公司以具竞争性的价格尽快地装运报盘,我方可大量地出售贵公司的货物。

请提供贵公司可供出口的产品的所有相关信息。

谨上

Ⅵ. Letter writing.

Write a letter to a foreign company for establishing business relations covering the following contents.

(1) source of the information about the foreign company;

(2) your intention to write the letter;

(3) self-introduction;

(4) reference as to your company's financial standing;

(5) your expectation.

Further Reading
扩展阅读

Letter 4: Letter from a Buyer

Dear Sirs,

We owe your name and address to the Chamber of Commerce of Shanghai who has informed us that you export the sportswear exclusively to Asia and your goods meet our demands. We are now writing to you in the hope of entering into business relations with you on the basis of equality and mutual benefit.

Our company has been importing sportswear for many years. There is always a ready market here for such goods, provided they are of good quality and competitive prices.

Since we are interested in doing business with your company, we would like to have some information about your company and your products. We would appreciate it if you can send us your catalogue and the latest price list.

You can know more of our information by going into our website. As to our credit standing, please refer to Bank of China, Shanghai Branch.

We look forward to your early reply with much interest.

Yours faithfully,

Letter 5: Letter from an Importer

Dear Sirs,

Subject: Hope to Establish Business Relations

The Bank of America has recommended your company as being interested in establishing business relations with a Chinese company for the purpose of exporting various products of your country and importing Chinese manufactured goods.

We specialize in trading with North American companies, but we have had no contact with your company. We send this order to you in order to ascertain whether cooperation to the advantage of both companies could be established. Please refer to the attachment for the detailed introduction of our company.

We invite you to send us the details and prices for such goods as you would be able to sell. We shall be glad to study the sales possibilities in our market.

Besides, please favor us with a list of those articles you are interested in obtaining from us, so that we might give you all the necessary information regarding supply possibilities.

Your early reply will be greatly appreciated.

Yours sincerely,

Encl.

Letter 6: Letter from an Exporter

Dear Sirs,

We write to introduce ourselves as one of the largest exporters, from China, of a wide range of Machinery and Equipment.

We enclose a copy of our latest catalogue covering the details of all the items available at present, and hope some of these items will be of interest to you.

It will be a great pleasure to receive your inquiries for any of the items against which we will send you our lowest quotations.

Should, by chance, your corporation not deal with the import of the goods mentioned above, we would be most grateful if this letter could be forwarded to the correct import corporation.

We are looking forward to your favorable and prompt reply.

Yours faithfully,

Encl.

Tips

Establishing Business Relations

A company may receive dozens or hundreds of business letters requesting for establishing business relationship. The letter for establishment of business relations should be answered without delay. Of course, not every letter can get a positive reply. Therefore, the reply to such letters can be classified into two kinds: a positive reply and a negative reply. Then how to write a proper reply becomes essential to a company to maintain the good image and the potential for future cooperation. Whether the reply is positive or negative, it should be courteous and sincere, and often include the following contents:

(1) Express thanks to the letter received.

(2) If the addresser wants to accept the other party's request, he should provide the other party with the information required; if the addresser wants to refuse the other party's request, he should express regret with courtesy and state the reasons for refusal.

(3) Express the hope of establishing business relations immediately or the desire for future cooperation.

Chapter 4 Enquiries
询盘

Learning Objectives

- Learn the basic contents involved in an enquiry letter
- Understand the difference between general enquiries and specific enquiries
- Master the writing steps about an enquiry letter

学习目标：了解询盘信涉及的基本内容，以及综合询盘与具体询盘的区别，掌握询盘信的写作步骤。

Case Study

After FG received the letter from Jin Yuan Corp. for the establishment of business relations, they obtained the general information about Jin Yuan Corp. through other sources. Later they found mulberry silk textile was well accepted in their local market. So they decided to enquire for such product.

Question: What should be contained in such a letter?

Introduction

An enquiry is a request for information regarding the goods, services or the terms and conditions. In general, it can be made by the seller or the buyer. If the enquiry is made by the buyer, it is called a bid. If the enquiry is made by the seller, it is called an invitation to make a bid.

Normally the enquirer should state clearly and concisely the general information he wants, such as a catalogue, a price list, a sample or specific demand for purchasing certain products such as price, quantity, port of shipment. For an enquiry from a regular customer, it sometimes only indicates the name of the commodity. For the first enquiry, the enquirer should indicate the source of information about the addressee, in addition to his own business scope, his history, etc.

A reply to the enquiry should be made promptly and answer all the questions mentioned. If samples are needed by the enquirer, they should be sent as soon as possible.

Specimen Letters

样信

Letter 1: Enquiry from FG

Dear Mr. Sun,

We acknowledge with thanks the receipt of your e-mail of Dec. 21. As an exporter of textiles, you are interested in establishing business relations with us. It is also our wish.

We are interested in the mulberry silk textile (silk yarn containing 85% or less, and other blended) in your catalogue, and shall be glad to receive your best quotation for 20,000 pieces of this **item**, with indication of detailed specifications, package and **terms of payment**. Please **offer** us CIF Marseilles.

We are awaiting your early reply.

Yours faithfully,

Letter 2: General Enquiry

Dear Sirs,

We have been informed by the Commercial Counselor's Office in your country that you are one of the **leading** exporters of light industrial products in China and that you wish to export air conditioners to our market.

We are pleased to make a self-introduction that our corporation is one of the major importers of air conditioners having over 20 years' history and enjoys high reputation in this line.

We would **be obliged** if you will send us your recent catalogues and price list. We believe that we will **place considerable orders** with you if the quality of your products is fine and the prices are reasonable.

Yours faithfully,

Letter 3: Enquiry from a Seller to a Buyer

Dear Sir or Madam,

Your firm has been recommended to us by ABC Company, New York, with whom we have done business for ten years.

We **specialize in** exportation of Chinese textiles, which have **enjoyed favorable reputation** all over the world. We enclose a copy of our **latest** catalogue **for your reference** and hope that you would be free to contact us if you are interested in any item.

We are looking forward to your early reply.

Yours faithfully,

Encl.

Letter 4: Specific Enquiry

Dear Sirs,

Re: Parts for Laser Printer S-2000

We purchased from you 200 sets of the **captioned** machine in 2025. We are glad that they have been quite satisfactory.

At present, we are **in the market for** the parts of accessories in a large quantity as per the enclosed list. Would you please quote the best CIF Lagos?

As there is an urgent demand for the parts and accessories, we hope to receive your reply by fax.

Yours faithfully,

Encl.

Letter 5: Specific Enquiry from an Importer

Dear Sirs,

We are glad to note from your letter of 1st March that you, as exporters of Chinese cotton piece goods, are willing to establish direct business relations with us, which happens to coincide with our desire.

At present, we are interested in printed shirting and shall be pleased if you will kindly send us by airmail the catalogues, sample books and other necessary information regarding printed shirting so as to acquaint us with the material and workmanship of your suppliers. Meanwhile, please quote us the lowest price CIF Lagos, inclusive of 5% commission, stating the earliest date of shipment. Should your price be found competitive and delivery date acceptable, we intend to place a large order with you.

Your early reply will be highly appreciated.

Yours faithfully,

Letter 6: E-mail from an exporter to a potential customer

To:

Cc:

From:

Subject: Re: Plastic Bottle with good quality

Dear John,

Glad to get your e-mail address on www.alibaba.com.

We supply all kinds of plastic bottles worldwide with good quality and moderate price.

As I surf on your official website, I found that you have built some chain stores in US. It is our pleasure if we can cooperate with you.

Here attached are some photos for our hot-selling items for your reference. Free samples could be sent on request.

Best Regards,

Words and Phrases 词汇

1. item n. (商品的)品种,条款,款项

This is the best-selling item in this line.

这是这类商品中的畅销货。

Item Two of the contract should be omitted.

合同的第二条应该删去。

There are several items of commission not yet paid.

尚有几笔佣金未支付。

2. specification n. 产品规格

Specifications: white color with size ranges from 35 to 40

规格:白色,尺寸 35—40

All details of specification of the product are written in this pamphlet.

该产品规格的详细资料可参见小册子。

3. terms of payment 支付条件,支付方式,付款条件

类似的表述有:payment terms, mode of payment, method of payment 付款方式

4. offer n. 报盘(包括货名、数量、规格、价格、船期、有效期等,通常和介词for/of/on 连用)

Please make us an offer CIF London for/on 20 metric tons of groundnuts.

请给我们报盘,20 公吨花生,CIF 伦敦价。

The offer is firm (valid, good, open, effective) for two weeks.

该报盘有效期两周。

A Japanese seller has made us an offer at US $ 130 per metric ton.

一位日本的卖方给我们报盘,每公吨 130 美元。

We are working on your offer of 200 kilos green tea.

我们正在研究贵方 200 千克绿茶的报盘。

offer v. 报盘

If you can offer, please telex us.

如果贵方能报盘,请电告我们。

At present, we cannot offer more than 1,000 short tons.

目前,我们的报盘不能超过 1 000 短吨。

5. be obliged 感激

We should be much obliged if you would inform us, in confidence, of their financial standing and modes of business.

如果贵方能告知我们他们的财务状况和业务模式,我们将不胜感激。

6. place regular orders 向某人定期订货

We shall place regular orders with you if your quality is fine and the price is moderate.

如果贵方的品质优良、价格适中,我们将定期订货。

7. specialize in 专门经营某一方面

be specialized in 专门经营

We are pleased to inform you that we have specialized in a variety of cotton piece goods for 20 years.

我们很高兴地告知贵方,我们专营各类棉布已有 20 年。

We are specialized in manufacturing automobile parts and industry parts.

我们专门从事汽车零配件和工业零配件的生产。

8. enjoy favorable reputation 享有盛誉

类似的表述有:enjoy great popularity, enjoy fast sales, enjoy a high reputation

Our black tea has enjoyed favorable reputation/has enjoyed a high reputation in the world market.

我们的红茶在世界市场上享有很好/很高的信誉。

Our goods enjoy fast sales.

我们的产品销路很好。

9. latest a. 最新的

Please send us your latest pricelist.

请给我们贵方最新的价目单。

10. for your reference 供贵方参考

类似的表述有:for your consideration, for your information

For your reference, the market for the leather is firm.

供贵方参考,皮革市场很坚挺。

11. captioned a. 标题项下的,标题所说的

the captioned article 标题货物,标题商品

We are glad to conclude a deal for the captioned article.

我们很高兴就标题项下的货物达成交易。

caption n. 标题

We received your letter of June 5, under the caption of L/C No. 433.

我们收到贵方 6 月 5 日的来信,标题为第 433 号信用证。

12. in the market for 想要购买

We are informed by ABC Company that you are in the market for Chinese black tea.

ABC 公司告知我们贵方想购买中国红茶。

in the market 要买或要卖

Please cable us as soon as you are in the market.

一旦贵方想要买或卖(某物),请电告我们。

good market 畅销

There is a good market for these articles.

这些商品很畅销。

find a ready market 畅销,有好销路

You can find a ready market for Chinese green tea here.

你们会发现中国绿茶在本地很畅销。

13. as per 按照,根据

As per your request, we are enclosing you a copy of our recent catalogue.

按照贵方要求,我们随附一份最新的商品目录。

14. hot-selling 热卖的

类似的表述有:top-rated, top-selling, the biggest-selling, best-selling

Useful Sentences 常用句型

1. Some of our clients show interest in your products and wish to have your quotations.

我们一些客户对贵方的产品感兴趣,希望获得贵方的报价。

2. We are an importer of woolen blankets and would like to obtain a catalogue and pricelist together with the samples as soon as possible.

我们是毛毯的进口商,希望能尽快获得商品目录、价目单以及样品。

3. We learn from our local Chamber of Commerce that you are dealing in various kinds of carpet and we shall be pleased if you can send us the price list and catalogues showing detailed information on the carpet you can supply.

我们从本地商会了解到贵方经营各类地毯,如果贵方能给我们提供带有详细信息的价格表和目录,我们将很高兴。

4. If the goods can be supplied from stock, please make us a firm offer on FOB basis.

如果货物可供现货,请给我们报实盘,FOB 价。

5. We would like to know if you could grant us a discount of 5% for the repeat orders.

我们想知道贵方能否给予我们的续订单 5%的折扣。

6. We should be obliged if you would kindly quote us your best price and state your best terms and discounts allowable.

如果贵方能给我们报最好的价格、条款和所能允许的折扣,我们将非常感激。

7. If the prices quoted are competitive and the quality up to standard, we will place orders on a regular basis.

如果所报价格具有竞争力,质量达到标准,我们将定期订货。

8. We should be much obliged if you could quote us the best CIFC 5% Shanghai and indicate the quantities and various sizes that you could supply for prompt shipment.

如果贵方可以给我们报最好的 CIF 上海价(含佣 5%),并提供贵方可以即期装运的数量和规格,我们将非常感激。

9. Please let us know on what terms you can supply the above goods.

请告知我们贵方能按什么条款供应上述商品。

10. We would appreciate it if you will let us know the ruling prices of the goods.

如果贵方能告知我们该商品的现行价格,我们将不胜感激。

11. As there is a growing demand for this type of equipment, we have to request for a special discount.

由于对这类设备的需求不断增加,我们想要一个特别折扣。

12. Please send us your best offer indicating packing, specifications, quantity available and the earliest time of delivery.

请给我们报包括包装、规格、可供数量及最早的交货时间在内的贵方最好的价格。

Exercises 练习

Ⅰ. Fill in the blanks with the proper word.

Dear Sirs,

We have learned ____ Company of Birmingham that you ____ a range of fashionable handbags in a variety of leathers.

We are one of the ____ retail traders here and although our sales volume is not ____, we ____ a good reputation in the ____ area.

Would you please ____ us a copy of your handbag catalogue ____ with details of your prices and payment ____?

We would find it most ____ if you could also ____ samples of different qualities of material ____ which the handbags are made.

Yours faithfully,

Ⅱ. Translate the following sentences into Chinese.

1. If you can supply products enquired for, we may place regular orders for large quantities.

2. When quoting, please state terms of payment and quantity discount you would allow, since we usually place substantial orders.

3. We would appreciate your sending us the latest samples together with their best prices.

4. To acquaint you with the electronic products we handle, we are sending you by separate airmail several pamphlets for your reference.

5. We will appreciate it highly if you airmail the catalogue and pricelist of the goods available at present.

6. We are large dealers in textiles and believe there is a promising market in our area for moderately priced goods of the kind mentioned.

7. When replying, please state terms of payment and discounts you would allow on purchases of quantities of not less than fifty dozen of individual items.

8. We now prefer to purchase from your company, because we are given to understand you are able to supply large quantities at more attractive prices.

9. Your lowest quotations are requested, by return, for the under-mentioned goods.

10. We are very well connected with all the major dealers here of light industrial products and feel sure we can sell large quantities of Chinese goods if we get your offers at competitive prices.

Ⅲ. Translate the following sentences into English.

1. 我们对贵公司生产的女式衬衫感兴趣,请告知能否提供现货。
2. 请告知贵公司对于数量在100公吨以上的订单能否给予3%的折扣。
3. 求购洗衣机,请寄带价目表的商品目录以供我们参考。
4. 请详细告知贵公司经营的主要商品情况及成交条件。
5. 我方有意进口贵方的产品,若能寄来目录、样品及价格单我们将不胜感激。
6. 我方相信贵方会对此询盘予以重视并及早答复。
7. 如您能告知该商品的现行价格,我方将不胜感激。
8. 请提供在花样和质量上与随函所附样品最相似的人造丝手帕样品。
9. 鉴于我方市场对此类设备的需求日增,务必请贵方考虑给予特别折扣。
10. 如果贵方运来的第一批货令人满意,随后将有大批续订。

Ⅳ. Translate the following letter into Chinese.

Dear Sirs,

We are interested in the new filing cabinets advertised by you in the current issue of the *Office Equipment* magazine, and we should like some more information.

At present we are using the drawer type filing cabinets and we should like to know:

1. If the new system is easier and quicker to operate?
2. How many files can be stored in each cabinet?
3. What is the capacity of each file?

Our present office furniture is light grey and we should like to match it as closely as possible. Could you let us see samples of the colors available?

We should be grateful to receive a prompt reply as we are in the process of replanning our filing system throughout the firm.

Yours faithfully,

V. Translate the following letter into English.

敬启者:

事由:型号 KG121 的报刊印刷机

关于我们上月在上海举行的华交会上的业务洽谈,我方现想询问一下贵方是否可以在成本加运保费到波士顿的基础上报给我方 200 台型号为 KG121 的报刊印刷机的实盘。

因我方客户急需这种型号的机器,若贵方能对此询盘予以即刻关注,我们当不胜感激。

谨上

VI. Letter writing.

Write a letter based on the given particulars.

Suppose you are working at ABC Import & Export Corp which desires to import some kitchen wares from French. You are required to write an enquiry letter to a French company to obtain the information about a quotation, a catalogue, discount, terms of payment and if possible, the samples.

Further Reading

扩展阅读

Letter 7: Specific Enquiry from an Importer

Dear Sirs,

We are now in the market for artificial leather gloves in bulk quantities and shall appreciate it if you will provide the following information about your products:

1. Details of your various types of gloves, including sizes, colors, prices and samples of different quality of materials used.

2. Your best quotation FOB Guangzhou, showing full particulars as to specifications and time of delivery.

3. Please also send two copies of descriptive literature.

Due to intense competition in the market, it is important that your quotation should reach us by end May so as not to miss this business opportunity.

We are looking forward to your earliest reply.

Yours faithfully,

Letter 8: Enquiry about a Company

Sinochem Jiangsu Import and Export Corporation
Jiangsu International Business Mansion
50 Zhonghua Road, Nanjing
210001, P. R. China

March 25th, 2025

China Construction Bank
Beijing Branch
Beijing, China

Dear Sirs,

As we are on the point of executing a considerable order from Messrs. J. A. Husman Co., P. O. Box 386, Karachi, we should be much obliged if you would inform us, in confidence, of their financial standing and modes of business.

The reference they have given us is the Standard Chartered Bank, Karachi Branch. Will you please be good enough to approach the said bank for all possible information we require?

It goes without saying that any information you may obtain for us will be treated in the strictest confidence and you are free from any responsibility.

We thank you in advance.

Yours faithfully,
Sinochem Jiangsu Import and Export Corporation

Letter 9: Favorable Reply

China Construction Bank

Beijing Branch

March 30th, 2025

Sinochem Jiangsu Import and Export Corporation
Jiangsu International Business Mansion
50 Zhonghua Road, Nanjing
210001, P. R. China

Dear Sirs,

In reply to your letter of March 25th, 2025, we wish to inform you that we have now received from the Standard Chartered Bank, Karachi Branch, the information you required.

J. A. Husman Co., P. O. Box 386, Karachi, was established in 1979 with a capital of Stg. 1,000. They major in the import and export of machines and electrical equipments. Their suppliers' business with them is reported to have been satisfactory. We consider them good for small business engagement up to an amount of Stg. 3,000. For large transactions we suggest payment by sight L/C.

The above information is strictly confidential and given without any responsibility on this bank.

Yours faithfully,

China Construction Bank, Beijing Branch

Tips

Enquiry

Business negotiation is an important part of conducting a deal. It is the dealings between the seller and the buyer in order to reach an agreement on price, payment, quantity, quality and other terms and conditions of a sale. Business negotiations are carried out either by writing or verbally. When business negotiation is done by writing, communications by letter, by fax or by e-mail are the usual means traders use.

To reach an agreement of the various terms in the business negotiation, in most cases, five stages or links are required: enquiry, offer, counter-offer, acceptance and conclusion of a contract. Of course, it is not necessary to have all the five steps taken for every transaction. Sometimes, only offer and acceptance will do. It is stipulated in the laws of some countries that only offer and acceptance are the two required factors, failure of which will make no contract.

An enquiry can be made not only to one party but also to several clients. In this way the enquirer can make a comparison between the terms of sales stated in the different replies and thus trade beneficially with the one who has quoted or offered the best terms.

Response must be sent immediately in the same way as the inquiry is sent. If quotations cannot be sent immediately, acknowledge the enquiry without delay to show efficiency and sincerity. Each enquiry is a sales opportunity to foster the potential long-term relationship.

Credit Enquiry

In business, "credit" commonly means the seller's faith and belief in the buyer's ability to pay for goods within a specified time after they have been delivered to them.

The buyer's credit mainly depends upon the following three respects: his character, capacity and capital. Character means his honesty, his industry, his moral conduct, his reputation for uprightness and fair play. His capacity is measured by his business experience, judgment and ability. Judgment of capacity will include such matters as the kind of business in which he is engaged, and the volume of business done. Capital situation refers to financial standing. Is the firm adequately capitalized? Has the firm sufficient working capital to carry on his business? Capital is the buyer's actual wealth, his liquid assets, his equity in building and equipment, and the ratio between his assets and liabilities. Based on a buyer's credit status, a seller makes a decision on whether he gives credit to buyer or how long and how much the credit will be.

In today's business world, the competition faced by sellers is becoming fiercer. It is obvious that doing business on credit terms is favorable to buyers since it will not tie up buyer's capital. In order to promote trade and increase the volume of business, sellers have to consider buyers' request for credit when negotiating business.

Before dealing with buyers' request for credit, sellers should first of all get references from buyers (applicant for credit). Usually the name of a bank, insurance company, or business acquaintance is given as a reference. Then the seller sends a letter to those references, requesting credit information about the buyer. The letter to reference should be compact, specific and courteous.

Responses to such enquiries are either favorable or unfavorable. However, in all cases the addresser (the reference) should phrase his letter so as to avoid any responsibility, either expressed or implied.

Chapter 5 Offers
报盘

Learning Objectives

- Master the definition of an offer
- Understand the differences between a firm offer and a non-firm offer
- Be familiar with the basic contents of an offer
- Grasp the steps in a letter on how to make an offer

学习目标：掌握报盘的定义；理解实盘和虚盘的区别；熟悉报盘的基本内容；掌握报盘信件的写作步骤。

Case Study

After Jin Yuan Corp. received the enquiry from FG, they contacted the domestic suppliers. After studying the quotations made by the domestic suppliers, Jin Yuan Corp. decided to deal with Jia Mei Textile Company. Based on the quotation from Jia Mei Textile Company, Jin Yuan Corp. made an offer to FG. What could be included in the offer?

Introduction

An offer is a proposal of terms and conditions presented in a potential contract by one party, called the offeror, to another party, called the offeree.

There are two kinds of offer: offer with engagement and offer without engagement.

In an offer with engagement, the offeror's intention of making a contract is definitely indicated, and the offeror cannot revoke or amend what he has offered during the validity of the offer. Normally it provides a term of validity. It can be defined as firm offer.

In brief, a firm offer with clarity and precision should contain the following points: the detailed description of the item, the price, the packaging, the minimum or the maximum quantity, the quality, the shipping date, the shipping mode, terms of payment and a timeframe during which the offer is valid.

Contrary to an offer with engagement, an offer without engagement is unclear, incomplete and with reservations. It usually expresses reservation, such as "subject to our final confirmation" "subject to goods being unsold" "only for reference".

The letter of an offer is usually organized in the following steps:

(1) Express thanks for the enquiry, if possible, making reference to the date or reference number.

(2) Indicate the nature of the offer, a firm offer or a non-firm offer. If it is a firm offer, state the period of validity. Otherwise, state it is an offer without engagement.

(3) State clearly the terms of commodity, quality, quantity, details of prices, shipment terms and terms of payment.

(4) If possible, make comments on the commodities or provide some additional information such as sample or catalogue enclosed or the special discount.

(5) Express expectation for an order or further cooperation.

Specimen Letters
样信

Letter 1: Offer from Jin Yuan to FG

Dear Mr. Brown,

Thank you for your enquiry for 20,000 pieces of mulberry silk textile. **As requested**, we contacted our suppliers and are pleased to offer you as follows:

Description of the goods: mulberry silk textile
silk yarn containing 85% or less and other blended

Packing: in export carton of 50 pieces each, indicating net weight 4 kilograms and gross weight 5 kilograms

Quantity: 20,000 pieces

Quality: 2024 crop

Price: USD 2.55 per piece CIF Marseille

Payment: **by letter of credit at sight**

This offer expires on or before January 15th, 2025. As the stock is limited, please send us your favorable reply in case this offer meets with your requirements.

Looking forward to receiving your early reply.

Best Regards

Lion Li

Sales Manager

JIN YUAN IMPORT AND EXPORT CO., LTD.

Letter 2: Non-firm Offer

Dear Sirs,

Re: Inquiry of Deerskin Handbags

Thank you for your letter of May 5th, in which you asked us to **inform** you of the price, the quantity available at present and the time of shipment.

Enclosed please find one copy each of our classified catalogues and the **samples.** To help you have a better understanding of our products, we are offering you **as follows, subject to our final confirmation:**

Description of the goods: deerskin handbags, Item No. MB12

Quantity: 300 dozen **available** at present

Unit Price: US $ 140 per dozen CIF Singapore

Time of Shipment: during August/September this year

Payment: **by letter of credit payable against draft at sight**

We hope you will find the above satisfactory. If you have any questions, please do not hesitate to approach us.

Yours faithfully,

Encl.

Letter 3: Non-firm Offer

Dear Sirs,

We acknowledge your enquiry of April 4th and thank you for your interest in our washing machines.

Our products are **of fine quality and moderate prices.** So we are pleased to quote you US \$ 180 per set CIF New York. Payment should be made by **sight**, **confirmed L/C in our favor.**

Please note that there is no **commission** on our products, but a **discount** of 3% is granted for the orders of 500 sets and up.

We hope you will find our quotation **acceptable** and look forward to your early reply.

Yours faithfully,

Letter 4: Firm Offer

Dear Sirs,

As requested in your letter of May 5th, we send you an offer as follows, subject to your reply reaching here not later than May 15th.

We offer firm 500 metric tons of wheat at USD × net per M/T CIF Singapore for shipment during August/September this year. We require payment by confirmed letter of credit available by draft at sight. This offer expires on or before May 15th.

Please note that this is the best offer we can make at present and we are unable to **entertain any counter-offer.** As you may know, there has been lately a strong **demand** for the commodities, so we trust that you will accept this offer.

We are looking forward to receiving your **fresh order.**

Yours faithfully,

Letter 5: Special Offer

Dear Sirs,

Men's Bicycles

We confirm your letter of May 20th, in which you asked us to send you an offer for the captioned bicycles. **At your request**, we are making you the following offer subject to your reply here within one week from the date of the letter.

Commodity: Men's Bicycles

Specification: 28′

Quantity: 300 sets

Price: US $ 200 per set FOBC3 Hamburg

Shipment: within one month after receipt of your L/C

Payment: by confirmed, irrevocable L/C payable against draft at sight received by the seller not later than July 30th

As you are aware, there has been active demand for bicycles in the market. Therefore, it is impossible for us to keep the offer open too long. Please take advantage of the present situation and send us an order early.

Yours truly,

Letter 6: E-mail for an Offer for MP4

To:

Cc:

From:

Subject: Re: Quote for MP4

Dear John,

Concerning your inquired item, newly developed Numan MP4, M6000, please check our offer as follows:

Item: MP4

Spec: M6000

Color: black, white, blue

Quantity: 200 dozen

FOB price: US $ 55/set

Samples could be prepared in 3 working days. Should you have interest in samples, please send us your address in detail with courier account.

Looking forward to your reply soon.

Best Regards,

Words & Phrases 词汇

1. non-firm offer/indefinite offer 虚盘

offer v. 报价,报盘

offer sth. to sb. ,offer for sth. ,offer sb. sth. 对……报价

offer n. 报价

与 offer 有关的短语:make an offer for 对……报盘(报价),send/forward an offer 寄送报盘,cable/telegraph an offer 电报报价,accept an offer 接受报盘,submit an offer 提交报盘, official offer 正式报价

We are ready to sell A.

我们打算出售 A。

We offer A, Shipment July, CIF London sterling 500 per metric ton.

我们报盘:商品 A,7 月份装运,每公吨 500 英镑,CIF 伦敦价。

We offer...subject to our final confirmation.

我们报盘……,以我方最后确认为准。

We make you an offer subject to the goods being unsold.

我们给贵方报盘,以货物未被售出为准。

We submit you this offer subject to prior sale.

我们给贵方报盘,货物先来先得。

We offer you subject to change without notice.

我们给贵方报盘,若有变动恕不通知。

2. firm offer 实盘

We offer you firm subject to reply by 5 p. m. our time, Wednesday, 3rd Oct.

我们给贵方报实盘,以 10 月 3 日,星期三,我方时间下午 5 点前贵方答复为准。

We offer you firm subject to reply reaching us by 10 a. m. , Tuesday our time.

我们给贵方报实盘,以贵方答复在星期二,我方上午 10 点前到此地为准。

We offer you firm subject to your reply here within one week from today.

我们给贵方报实盘,以贵方答复自今日起一周内到此地为准。

firm a. 确定的,有效的

The offer is firm/good/open/valid effective(for) 3 days.

该报盘的有效期为 3 天。

This is a firm offer.

这是一个实盘。

3. as requested 按照要求

类似的表述有:as was requested, as it was requested, at your request, as per your request 按贵方要求的

Enclosed please find some sample books as requested.

请查收按贵方要求随附的一些样本册。

4. By letter of credit payable against draft at sight 以即期信用证方式付款

类似的表述有:letter of credit available by draft at sight, letter of credit payable against draft at sight, letter of credit available by sight draft, letter of credit payable against sight draft, sight L/C, L/C at sight 即期信用证

5. inform v. 通知,告诉,报告

inform sb. of sth. 告知某人某事

Please inform us of the market situation on your side.

请告知我们贵方的市场状况。

inform sb. that/what/which 告知某人……

Please inform us what quantity you can purchase per year.

请告知我们贵方每年的订货量。

Please be informed that...特此通知……

Please be informed that we have already sent the sample required.

特此告知我们已经寄出贵方所要的样品。

keep sb. informed of/that 随时告知

We hope you will keep us informed of the market condition at your end.

希望贵方能随时告知我们贵方的市场状况。

6. sample n. 样品(后接介词 of 或 for)

We have forwarded you under separate cover two samples for this article.

我们已另邮给贵方该产品的两份样品。

We must stress that the sample is for your reference only.

我们必须强调样品仅供参考。

7. as follows, as what follows 如下

It is as follows:

内容如下:

The telegrams read as follows:

电报内容如下:

We state as follows:

我们声明如下:

8. subject to our final confirmation 以我们最后确认为准

subject to... 在……条件下,以……为条件

We offer 100 M/T Bitter Apricot Kernels at RMB... CIF..., prompt shipment, subject to our cable confirmation.

我们为苦杏仁报价,100 公吨,人民币××,CIF××,即期装运,以我方电报确认为准。

This quotation is subject to our further confirmation.

该报价以我方进一步确认为准。

Subject to your shipment in May, we will order 5,000 metric tons.

如果贵方5月份装运,我们将订5 000公吨,

9. available a. 可利用的,可供应的

We will ship by the first steamer available (the first available steamer) next month.

下个月我们将通过能利用的首条船只安排装运。

This is the only stock available (the only available stock).

这是仅有的可供存货。

10. time of shipment 装运时间

类似的表述有:time of delivery, delivery time, date of delivery, delivery date, date of shipment, shipment time, shipment date 装船期,交货期

11. of fine quality and moderate price 品质良好,价格适宜

be of good quality = the quality is good 质量上乘

be of moderate price = the price is moderate 价格适中

12. commission n. 佣金

a commission of 5%　5%的佣金

two items of commission 两笔佣金

The above price includes your 2% commission.

上述价格包括贵方2%的佣金。

13. acknowledge v. 告知收到,常用于国际商务信函的起始句

We acknowledge receipt of your letter of June 14th.

我们收到贵方6月14日的来信。

14. in sb.'s favor 有利于某人,(信用证等)以某人为受益人

The current exchange rate is in your favor.

现行汇率对贵方有利。

We hereby open an irrevocable L/C in your favor to the amount of US $ 30,000 for account of ABC Company.

兹开立以ABC公司为开证申请人、贵方为受益人的信用证,金额为3万美元。

in favor of 赞成,主张

They are in favor of free trade.

他们主张自由贸易。

15. discount n. 折扣,贴现,减价

quantity discount 数量折扣, special discount 特殊折扣, cash discount 付现折扣

allow/give/make/grant a ××% discount off/on the prices of goods 按货价给予××%的折扣

The highest discount we can allow (give/make/grant) on this article is 10%.

我们对该商品所能给予的最高折扣为10%。

We give 10% discount for cash payment.

对于现金付款,我们予以九折优惠。

The rate of discount in London is now 5%.

当前伦敦的贴现率为5%。

at a discount 低于正常价格,打折扣

The goods are selling at a discount.

该商品正以低价销售。

16. acceptable adj. 可接受的,合意的

We shall place a large order for men's shirts with you, if the time of delivery is acceptable to us.

如果交货期可接受的话,我们将向贵方下一个男士衬衫的大订单。

17. entertain v. 接受,考虑

entertain any counter-offer 考虑还盘

We are too heavily committed to be able to entertain fresh orders.

我们任务太重,不能考虑新订单。

We shall be glad to entertain any constructive suggestion you may make.

我们将很乐意考虑贵方提出的任何建设性的提议。

18. demand n. 需求(后接介词 for)

There is little or no demand at present for this article.

当前对于该商品的需求很小或没有。

There is a large (strong) demand for these goods.

对于这些商品的需求很大。

As the demand has become softer, interest is cooling off.

由于需求比较疲软,(对该商品的)兴趣在降低。

The goods are in large (small/regular) demand.

对该商品的需求很大(很小、稳定)。

v. 需求,需要

The buyer demands that seller should ship 10,000 MT nails within a week.

买方要求卖方在一周内装运 1 万公吨钉子。

The buyer demands of the seller to ship the goods within a week.

买方要求卖方一周内装运货物。

active demand 畅销,需求活跃, articles in great demand 需求量很大的商品, payable on demand 见票即付, total demand 总需求

19. fresh order 新订单

At present we cannot entertain any fresh orders.

当前我们不考虑任何新订单。

20. courier account 快递账号

类似的表述有:express account, freight collect account

外贸行业里,一般问对方要快递账号,往往就表示让对方提供"到付账号"。

Please give me your FedEx account.

请提供一下您的联邦快递账号。

Useful Sentences 常用句型

1. As requested, we take pleasure in offering you, subject to our final confirmation, 300 dozen of blouses at US $ 150 per dozen CIF Singapore.

按照要求,我们很高兴给贵方报盘,300 打女士衬衫,每打 150 美元 CIF 新加坡,以我方最后确认为准。

2. In reply, we offer firm, subject to your reply reaching us on or before Sept. 20th for 100 metric tons of Groundnuts, Handpicked at RMB ¥2,000 net per metric ton CFR Copenhagen or any other European Main Ports.

作为答复,我们报实盘,以贵方答复 9 月 20 日或之前到达我方为准, 手拣

花生 100 公吨,每公吨净价人民币 2 000 元,CFR 哥本哈根或任何其他欧洲主要港口。

3. In order to start a concrete transaction between us, we take pleasure in making you a special offer, subject to our final confirmation, as follows...

为了开展我们之间的业务,我们很乐意给贵方一个优惠报盘,内容如下,以我方最后确认为准。

4. This offer must be withdrawn if not accepted within five days.

该报盘如果 5 天内不被接受,将会被撤销。

5. You will note that these quotations are open for a week only, because of the frequent fluctuation of the market price.

你们将会注意到,由于市场价格的频繁波动,这些报价的有效期仅限一周。

6. Please note that we have quoted our most favorable price and unable to entertain any counter offer.

请注意,我们所报的是很优惠的价格,因此不能够接受任何还盘。

7. In order to enlarge the volume of trade, we make an exceptionally lower price. We shall be unable to repeat it when our present stock is exhausted.

为了扩大贸易量,我们报了一个前所未有的低价。当目前存货销完后,我方将不再按此价格报盘。

8. We wish to state that our quotations are subject to alternation without notice and to our confirmation at the time of placing your order.

我们想申明一下,我们的报价若有变更恕不另行通知,并且以我方接受贵方订货时的确认为准。

9. We would like to let you know that we usually offer a 20% discount if the order is substantial. You can find the details on quantity discounts in the catalogue.

我们想告知贵方,如果订货数量大,我们通常提供 20%的折扣。贵方可以在商品目录中查阅数量折扣的详情。

10. We cabled back this morning, offering 50 metric tons of cotton at US $ ____ CIF Copenhagen for shipment during October 2025.

今天早上我们以电报回复,报盘 50 公吨棉花,____美元 CIF 哥本哈根,装运期为 2025 年 10 月。

11. We trust the above will be acceptable to you and await with keen interest your trial order.

我们相信上述报盘对贵方来说是可接受的,热切期待贵方的试订单。

Exercises 练习

Ⅰ. Fill in the blanks with the appropriate words.

Dear Sirs,

In answer to your recent enquiry____September 25th, 2025, we are ______the ____to offer____blouses.

Item No. ×× Blouse Size×× Colors×× Unit Price××($)

Prices are____FOB San Francisco basis. Terms of payment are____irrevocable documentary credit to be received one month____to the date of delivery. Discounts are 0.5% for orders of 100—500 pieces, and 1.5% for 500—1,000 pieces.

Each item is individually boxed with our company logo. All cartons are waterproof and standard for overseas shipment. Delivery is guaranteed to be____four weeks____receipt of L/C.

As you know our blouses are very popular, we are sure that your customers will continue to be satisfied with our products. We look____to receiving your prompt reply as the prices are____for only 10 days.

Sincerely yours,

Ⅱ. Translate the following sentences into Chinese.

1. As requested, we are offering you the following subject to our final confirmation.

2. Please kindly note that the offer is open for acceptance until the 12th of this month.

3. We trust that you will be able to accept our offer, which shall be kept open against reply by cable.

4. We were very pleased to receive your enquiry of 4th June and now confirm our

cable offer of this morning as follows.

5. As the market is firm with an upward tendency, we would suggest in your interest that you accept our offered price.

6. As we have no timbers in our stock, we regret that we are unable to offer.

7. Unless otherwise stated or agreed upon, all prices are net without commission.

8. On condition that you take more than 2,000 sets, we are prepared to offer this special price of US $ 10 per set, 3% discount.

9. We quote for this article at USD 10 per case FOB Shanghai.

10. As the prices quoted are exceptionally low and likely to rise, we would advise you to accept the offer without delay.

Ⅲ. Translate the following sentences into English.

1. 就贵方所提及的最新型号的产品,我们很高兴地向贵方报价如下。

2. 按照贵方的要求,我们报 50 公吨大豆的实盘如下,以自本日起一周之内贵方回复为准。

3. 如果贵方认为这一报盘可以接受,请即来电,以便我方确认。

4. 这些报价是随市场波动而变动的。

5. 我们能以具有吸引力的价格向贵方报各种各样的中国棉布。

6. 现回复贵方 10 月 2 日询盘,报 5 公吨核桃仁 CFR 汉堡价。

7. 我们希望贵方认同我方价格具有竞争力,因为我方服装质量优良。

8. 我方很高兴附上现行报价单一份供贵方参考,我方可即期交货,希望不久能收到贵方电报订单。

9. 我们是家用电器出口商,现冒昧给贵方寄去我们的报价单供选择。

10. 我方了解到贵方市场对运动衣需求强劲,借此良机,附上我方第 21 号报价单供贵方考虑。

Ⅳ. Translate the following letter into Chinese.

Dear Sirs,

We are pleased to have your enquiry of May 28th regarding the best quality Color

TV. You will be interested in our latest models which enjoy the most advanced technologies in Color TV. Meanwhile we can supply a three-year guarantee on replacement parts.

At present we are fully committed until the end of August. We shall be in a position to supply you with a maximum of 1,000 sets of each type per month, together with an adequate supply of spare parts.

For the details of our export prices and terms of payment, please refer to the enclosure. Our illustrated catalogue is being sent to you under separate cover soon.

We look forward to coming to terms with you.

Yours faithfully,

V. Translate the following letter into English.

敬启者:

很高兴收到贵方8月25日询价,根据贵方要求,今寄上有插图的目录和明细价目单。此外,另封邮寄一批样品。

相信贵方看到上述资料和样品后,定会同意我方产品质量上乘、价格合理。由于质地柔软、耐用,我们的全棉床单备受欢迎。贵方在研究我方价格之后,自然会感到我们难以满足市场需求的原因。

若贵方在本月底前下订单,我方可保证在收到订单后两周内交货。对定期购买不少于50打的商品,我方可给予5%的折扣。

请注意我方价目单上的其他产品,并盼早来首次订单。

谨上

Ⅵ. Letter writing.

Write a letter to ABC Company and make a firm offer for the Washing Machines.

Further Reading
扩展阅读

Letter 7: Firm Offer

Dear Sirs,

Thanks for your enquiry letter of May 4th for our sportswear. We are very glad to learn that we have an opportunity to conclude the deal for the above goods. As requested, we have already sent you under separate cover the samples and the illustrated catalogue. Now we offer the best price as follows:

Commodity: Men's Sportswear

Size: Large, Medium

Packing: each wrapped in a polythene bag and then 100 packed in a crate

Unit Price: USD 40 per piece net CIF Hamburg

Delivery: within one month after receipt of L/C

Minimum Quantity: 2,000 pieces

Payment: by 100% irrevocable credit available by draft at sight

Please note that the above offer is subject to your reply here on or before May 20th, Beijing time. We assure you that prompt attention will be surely drawn to your order.

Yours sincerely,

Letter 8: Non-firm Offer

Dear Sirs,

We thank you for your letter dated June 9th enquiring for leather handbags. At your request, we take pleasure in offering you, subject to our final confirmation, 300 dozen of deerskin handbags style No. 24 at USD 300 per dozen CIF Singapore. Shipment will be effected within one month after receipt of the relative L/C issued by your leading bank in our favor.

We are manufacturing various kinds of leather purses and waist-belts for exportation, and enclosed please find a brochure of our products. We hope some of them would meet your customers' requirement.

If we can be of any further help, please do not hesitate to approach us. Customers' enquiries always meet with our careful and prompt attention.

Yours truly,

Encl.

Letter 9: Exporter's Quotation

Dear Sirs,

We thank you for your enquiry of 23rd September for Silk 6311. While we appreciate your efforts in pushing the sale of our products, we very much regret that we are not in a position to offer you the desired quality, owing to excessive demand.

However, we should like to take this opportunity to offer without engagement the following material as a close substitute for your consideration: 500 pieces Silk 6103 at USD 4.8 per yard, CIF Hamburg, including your commission of 3%.

If you are able to close business as we propose here, please tell us as soon as possible.

Yours faithfully,

Tips

Offer

Like an enquiry, an offer can be made either by a seller or by a buyer. The offer made by the seller is customarily called "selling offer" with such wording as "can supply" "supply" "offer" in it, while the offer made by the buyer is commonly called "buying offer", in which a different word such as "book" "order" "bid" can be used. In general, it is the seller, not the buyer, who offers the sale of certain commodities to the buyer.

There are two kinds of offer: offer with engagement and offer without engagement.

In an offer with engagement, the offeror's intention of making a contract is definitely indicated, and the offeror cannot revoke or amend what he has offered during the validity of the offer. Once it is unconditionally accepted by the offeree within its validity, the transaction is completed and a contract is concluded right away, which is binding on both parties. Though named as a firm offer, it is not necessary to have "firm offer" or "offer firm" all the time in the offer. What is important is that a firm offer or an offer with engagement should be clear, complete and final in its wording. The word "To be clear" means that the intention and terms in the offer should be clearly described without ambiguity. The word "To be final" signifies that the offeror intends, without reservation, to enter into a contract with the offeree if all the terms offered are accepted by the offeree. The word "To be complete" means that the main trading terms including those about the name of the goods, quality and specifications, quantity, packing, price, delivery, and payment should be completely denoted.

An offer with engagement mostly provides a term of validity. In this case the offer remains valid until the validity ends. The acceptance made by the offeree before the validity expires is effective legally. However, there are different interpretations concerning this problem in different countries. A firm offer lapses when it exceeds the time limit because of passage of time, or when it is rejected or counter-offered.

In brief, a firm offer with clarity and precision should contain the following points: a detailed description of the item, price, packaging, minimum or maximum quantity, quality, shipping date, mode, terms of payment and a timeframe during which the offer is valid.

Contrary to an offer with engagement, an offer without engagement, is unclear, incomplete and with reservations. Such offer is not binding on the offeror with the following expressions "reference price" "subject to our final confirmation" "subject to being unsold". Generally speaking, quotation sheets and price lists serve as offers without engagement because they only include part of the terms, such as names, descriptions, specifications and unit prices. They do not include those terms about shipment, payment, etc. The main terms are not completely listed. Besides, the statements like "The prices are subject to change without notice" or "Subject to our final confirmation" inserted in quotation sheets and price lists make the offer not final.

According to the "United Nations Convention on Contracts for the international Sale of Goods", an offer becomes valid when it is received. An offer can only be withdrawn if the withdrawal reaches the offeree before or at the same time with the offer. Once an offer becomes valid, it can only be revoked before the acceptance is dispatched. However, if an offer itself states that it is irrevocable, it cannot be revoked.

Chapter 6 Counter-offers
还盘

Learning Objectives

- Understand the definition of counter-offer
- Grasp the steps in writing letters on counter-offer

学习目标:理解还盘的含义;掌握还盘信写作的步骤。

Case Study

After FG received the offer from Jin Yuan Corp, they found some terms were not satisfactory. Then they made a counter-offer. What could be involved in the counter-offer?

Introduction

If one party does not agree with any or some of the transaction terms of a quotation from another party, he can send a counter offer. In other words, a counter-offer is an offer made by one of the two parties, usually the buyer, in response to the previous offer. The original offeror now becomes the offeree and he has the right of acceptance or refusal. In the latter case, he may make another counter offer of his own. This process can go on for many rounds till business is finalized or called off. A counter-offer may be directed against the price, packing, shipment or other important trade terms.

In counter-offer letters, the seller or the buyer should clearly state his objections to certain terms and conditions offered. Meanwhile, he should give proper reasons to support his objections and preferably state his own proposals for conclusion of the transaction.

Normally such counter-offer letters cover the following points:

(1) Express the thanks for the offer;

(2) Express the regret for disagreement to certain terms and if possible, state the reasons for disagreement;

(3) Put forward possible suggestions or amendments to the offer;

(4) Express the desire to receive a favorable reply.

Specimen Letters

样信

Letter 1: Counter-offer from FG

Dear Mr. Li,

We are very grateful of receiving your offer together with the samples today.

While **appreciating** the fine quality of your goods, we find your price is rather higher than what we expected. We have to ask you to consider if you can make a reduction in your price. As our order would be around USD 2.20/pc, you may think it worthwhile to **make a concession.**

Your earlier reply will be highly appreciated.

Yours faithfully,

Letter 2: Counter-offer for a Lower Price

Dear Sirs,

Thank you for your offer of Aug. 5th. Although we appreciate the quality of your sewing machine and delivery date, the prices are too high to be accepted.

As per the S/C No. 3456, you will find that we **ordered** 1,000 sets of sewing machine **on the terms and conditions** stipulated in that **S/C**, except that the price was 10% lower than your present quotation. Since we placed the last order, prices for raw materials have been **decreased considerably**. In addition, the retailing prices for sewing machines here have been reduced by 15%. So it is impossible for us to accept your price.

We would like to **place repeat orders** with you if you could reduce your price at least by 3%. Otherwise we have to purchase the products from other suppliers.

We hope you take our suggestion into serious consideration and give us your favorable reply as soon as possible.

Yours faithfully,

Letter 3: Counter-offer for a Substitute

Dear Sirs,

We take pleasure in receiving your quotation of May 14th, hoping to place a repeat order with us for 2,000 sets of sewing machine, Model 31.

While we appreciate your offer, we regret that we cannot provide you with the model of **articles** at present owing to strong demand for the goods both at home and abroad. Would you like to consider Model 18 as a substitute which is very close to your choice in quality though slightly higher in price?

We await your favorable reply with great interest.

Yours faithfully,

Letter 4: Counter-offer for an Earlier Delivery

Dear Sirs,

We acknowledge with thanks your letter of May 8th, in which you offered us 4,000 dozen of men's shirts under FOB basis.

We find that your price is quite satisfactory. However, your time of shipment is too late to be acceptable as the busy season is approaching. If you cannot **see your way clear to** ensure that the goods will reach us to catch the selling season, we are afraid that we will have to cover our requirements elsewhere.

We await with keen interest your favorable reply.

Yours truly,

Letter 5: E-mail for a Counter-offer for Price

To:

Cc:

From:

Subject: Re: Price for Numan MP4, M6000

Dear John,

I am sorry we cannot accept your target price for Numan MP4, M6000 at US $ 50.5/set.

As I mentioned in the previous email, your target price leaves us little margin of profit on our sales. We could give you 2 dollars off as maximum. That means, US $ 53 US our floor price.

Please understand our situation and email back us.

Thank you!

Kind regards,

Words & Phrases 词汇

1. appreciate v. 理解;欣赏;感谢,感激;上涨

We hope that you can appreciate our situation.

我们希望贵方能够理解我们的处境。

We shall appreciate your giving this matter your serious consideration.

如果贵方能对这件事情认真地考虑,我们将非常感谢。

We shall appreciate it if you will send us your latest catalogue by air immediately.

如果贵方能以航空方式立即将最新的商品目录寄给我们,我们将不胜

感激。

Your prompt reply will be greatly appreciated.

如贵方尽快回复,我们将不胜感激。

The prices of the raw materials have appreciated.

原材料的价格已经上涨。

2. make a concession 做出让步

We agree to make a concession and grant you a reasonable compensation.

我们同意做出让步,给予贵方一个合理的补偿。

To conclude the deal, we really think we should make some concessions.

为达成交易,我们真的打算做些让步。

3. order n. 订单,订货,所订的货

v. 订购

名词 order 常与动词 make, send, place 等连用,表示订购某项货物,接介词 for, on, of

If your price is reasonable, we will send you an order for 2,000 pieces.

如果贵方价格合理,我们将下一个 2 000 件的订单。

We expect to ship your order next month.

我们期待下个月装运贵方订货。

If you grant us 5% discount, we will order 1,000 pieces.

如果贵方能给予我们 5%的折扣,我们将订货 1 000 件。

与 order 相关的短语:fresh order 新订单, initial order 首次订货, repeat order 续订单, duplicate order 重复订单, accept an order 接受订货, execute/fulfill/fill/carry out an order 执行订单, cancel an order 取消订单, withdraw an order 撤回订单

4. place repeat orders 重复订货

place an order with sb. 向某人订货

place a substantial/considerable order with sb. 向某人大量订购

We are glad to place an order with you for 2,000 sets of air conditioners.

我们很高兴向贵方订购 2 000 台空调。

We have pleasure in placing a repeat order as follows.

我们很高兴续订货，内容如下。

We wish to place considerable orders with you if your quality is fine and the prices reasonable.

如果贵方商品的品质好、价格合理，我们希望能大量订货。

We will place regular orders with your firm if your goods are of excellent quality.

如果贵公司产品质量好的话，我们会长期订货。

5. on the terms and conditions 按照条款

terms and conditions 条款，条件

terms 条件，用复数，主要指大的方面，如付款方式，conditions 往往指 terms 确定后的具体条件，如通过哪家银行开证。

All the terms and conditions shall be clearly and completely stated in the contract.

合同中应清楚完整地规定所有条款。

We cannot do business on your terms.

我们不能按照贵方的条件进行交易。

6. S/C, sales confirmation/sales contract 销售确认书/销售合同

The buyer is requested to countersign and return one copy of this sales confirmation immediately for our file.

买方被要求立即会签并退还一份售货确认书给我们以便我们存档。

In international trade, a sales confirmation is a document regarded as a contract.

在国际贸易中，售货确认书是被视为合同的文件。

7. decreased considerably 大幅度降低

8. article n. 商品

This article is quite best selling at present.

这类商品当前相当畅销。

9. see your way clear to 设法(做某事)

We trust that you will see your way clear to deliver the goods by end May.

我们相信贵方会在 5 月底前发货。

We cannot see our way (clear) to increase the quantity.

我们无法再增加数量。

10. floor price 地板价,最低价格

Useful Sentences 常用句型

1. We regret to say that we cannot accept your offer as your price is on the high side.

很遗憾,由于贵方的价格偏高,我们不能接受贵方的报盘。

2. In view of the market conditions here, we deem that your price is unrealistic and the price bid by us is the best you can obtain at present.

鉴于当前的市场形势,我们认为贵方的价格是不现实的,我方报价是贵方当前可以获得的最好价格。

3. Should you be prepared to reduce your price by 5%, we might come to terms with you.

如果贵方准备将价格降低5%,我们可能会和贵方达成交易。

4. We have cut our price to the limit. We regret, therefore, being unable to comply with your request for further reduction.

我们已将价格降低到极限。因此,我们很遗憾不能按照贵方的要求做更多减让。

5. We regret to inform you that we cannot accept your offer, as we are obtaining the same quality from other sources at a price 6% lower than yours.

很遗憾地告知贵方,我们不能接受贵方的报盘,因为我们可以从其他供货商处以低于贵方6%的价格获得同等品质的商品。

6. We would be willing to discuss a quantity discount if your order is doubled.

如果贵方的订货量增加一倍,我们愿意协商数量折扣。

7. Owing to heavy commitments, we regret that we cannot entertain any fresh orders for the captioned goods.

由于任务太多,我们很遗憾不能接受标题项下货物的任何新订单。

8. Your price is quite in line, but the time of shipment is too distant.

贵方的价格很合理,但交货期太长。

9. We can offer a substitute which is at the same price and of similar quality to the goods ordered.

我们能够对与所订商品价格相同、质量相近的替代品报盘。

10. Since our price is closely calculated, we regret being unable to grant the discount you asked for.

由于我们的价格是经过仔细计算得出来的,我们很遗憾无法满足贵方所提出的折扣要求。

11. We are regretful to say that our customers find your price is on the high side and out of line with the prevailing market.

很遗憾,我们的客户认为贵方的价格偏高,与当前的市场行情不相符合。

12. Though we find your price and quality satisfactory, we suggest that your terms of payment should be altered.

尽管我们发现贵方的价格和质量都令人满意,但我们建议贵方修改付款条件。

Exercises 练习

Ⅰ. Fill in the blanks with the proper words.

Dear Sirs,

We are____possession of your offer July 8th for Jinling Brand automatic washing machine USD 120 per set FOB Guangzhou____of our 5% commission.

While____the quality of your products, we____a careful study of your offer. We find your prices are too high to be____. In fact, the cost of raw materials has not____in the____three months. In order to make your products more____in our____, we suggest that you____price____10%. If you will agree to our counter-suggestion,____orders for large____will be placed. Otherwise, we will conduct our business elsewhere.

Please let us have your early____.

Yours faithfully,

Ⅱ. Translate the following sentences into Chinese.

1. Owing to shortage of stock, we regret that we are unable to accept your repeat

order.

2. If you could grant a concession of 3% on your quoted price, your price will be quite competitive.

3. We hope you will see your way to accept September shipment.

4. The highest discount we can allow on this article is 10%.

5. This is the rock-bottom price; therefore, we cannot make any further reduction.

6. We would like to comply with your request by lowering the price to US $ 30.00 per carton, but the minimum quantity for your order should be 100 metric tons.

7. If a substantial reduction can be expected, we could reconsider your revised quotation.

8. While we appreciate your cooperation in giving us an offer, we regret to say that we are not in the market for this commodity now.

9. Unless the prices could match with the market level, it is difficult for us to persuade our customers to purchase from you.

10. We can only accept your special offer if you assure improved packing of your goods.

Ⅲ. Translate the following sentences into English.

1. 我们不能接受贵方的报价,因为该报价让我们几乎无利可图。

2. 考虑到我们之间长期的良好合作关系,我们愿意在各让一步的基础上,即降价 5%,与贵方达成交易。

3. 我们非常遗憾地说,把价格降低到贵方所指的 15% 的程度是不可能的。

4. 实在对不起,对于此次贵公司的订货条件,我公司无法供货。

5. 目前,关于此类特制品没有存货,工厂也无法立即制造,因此,我们担心在接到订单后恐怕不能保证在 3 个月内交货,敬请谅解。

6. 非常抱歉,我们无法依从贵方对有关包装的特殊要求,但愿意提供如下的特别报价。

7. 由于我公司仓储能力的限制,货物需分 3 次发运。不知贵方能否接受这样的装运方式?

8. 感谢贵方寄来了棉织品货样,但现在我们对此没有兴趣。

9. 因为我方的原料供应在几个月前已分配给其他订单,故目前不能接受贵公司的订单。

10. 市价很可能会上涨,尽早订购对贵方有利。

Ⅳ. Translate the following letter into Chinese.

Dear Sirs,

Subject: Your offer for Sugar

We wish to thank you for your letter of 20th February, offering us for 50 long tons of the captioned goods at USD 105.00 per long ton CIF London, on usual terms.

In reply, we very much regret to state that our end-users here find your price too high and out of line with the prevailing market level. Information indicates that the sugar made in Britain have been sold at the level of USD 98.00 per long ton.

Such being the case, it is impossible for us to persuade our end-users to accept your price, as goods of similar quality are easily obtainable at a much lower price. Should you be prepared to reduce your limit by, say 8%, we might come to terms.

It is in view of our long-standing business relationship that we make you such a counter-offer. As the market is declining, we hope you will consider our counter-offer most favorably and fax us acceptance at your earliest convenience.

We are anticipating your early reply.

Yours faithfully,

Ⅴ. Translate the following letter into English.

敬启者:

很高兴收到贵方9月18日的来信,关于34英寸"长虹"彩色电视机的报盘,每台价格为450美元CIF哥本哈根。

作为答复,我们很遗憾地告知你们,贵方的价格太高了。市场行情表明,一些日本彩色电视机在此地的售价比贵方的价格大概低出了30%。

我们不否认"长虹"彩色电视机的品质,但价格差太大了。为促进交易,我们还盘如下,我们的订货量为1万台34英寸"长虹"彩色电视机,单价为430美元CIF哥本哈根。

希望你们能认真考虑此事,并尽早告知我们贵方的答复。

谨上

Ⅵ. Letter writing.

Suppose you are an importer of sewing machine and now receive an offer from a Chinese company. Please reply to the offer and ask for reduction of the price for the initial order, stating your reasons for the reduction and expressing the possibility of concluding the deal if the request for reduction is met with.

Further Reading
扩展阅读

Letter 6: Counter-offer for a Concession on the Price

Dear Sirs,

Thank you for making us the offer for canvas shoes so promptly.

In reply, we regret to inform you that the price you quoted is found too high. It leaves us no margin of profit. To set up the trade, we suggest that you make some concessions, say 10%, on your quoted price, and we feel confident that it will be helpful to push the sale of your goods in our area. If this proposal is acceptable to you, we shall place an order with you immediately.

We look forward to your favorable reply.

Yours faithfully,

Letter 7: Reply to the Above

Dear Sirs,

Canvas Shoes

We learn from your letter of 10th October that our price for the subject article is found to be on the high side.

Much as we would like to cooperate with you in expanding sales, we are regretful that we just cannot see our way clear to entertain your counter-offer, as the price we quoted is quite realistic. As a matter of fact, we have received a lot of orders from various sources at our level.

If you see any chance to do better, please let us know. On account of a limited supply available at present, we would ask you to act quickly.

In the meantime, please keep us posted of developments at your end. We assure you that any further enquiries from you will receive our prompt attention.

Yours faithfully,

Letter 8: Counter-offer on Delivery

Dear Sirs,

Thank you for your offer dated October 10th, 2025. As you know, your toys always sell well in our stores.

While appreciating other terms of your offer, we would hope that due to our long business relationship you could do better with the delivery. It is known that we are trying to put these items on the shelves before the Christmas season. Therefore, we hope to receive them as soon as possible and would ask if you could guarantee delivery within two weeks after receipt of the L/C. We then need time to distribute the goods to each chain store and get the items stocked.

Please let us know if you will be able to accept the delivery schedule.

We look forward to your immediate answer.

Yours sincerely,

Letter 9: Counter-offer on Quantity

Dear Sirs,

We are so pleased to receive your offer of April 25th, 2025. We have considered your offer carefully and are pleased with most of the terms.

We find the quantities in your offer to be on the small side. It is our custom to order at least 30 at a time, especially as this is the time that we prepare for our annual bedding sale. So, we would request that you be able to provide at least 30 of each item at a time.

We are most happy with your products and would not like to go to another supplier to meet our needs. So we hope that you will be able to increase the amount of each shipment to 30 each.

Please advise us within this week if this is acceptable so that we can draw up the contract as soon as possible and meet our timetable for the sale.

Yours sincerely,

Tips

Counter-offer

A counter-offer, in fact, is a rejection of the offer. It means the offeree does not accept the offer wholly and put forward some additions, modifications, limitations, etc. as to the basic terms and conditions contained in the offer. Hence, it is a new offer and at the same time, the original offer lapses. In a counter-offer a new price as well as the other new terms is suggested. When used, it is often simply worded with only the new suggested terms stated. In order to make certain that the other terms embodied in the original offer remain unchanged, the date and/or reference number of the original offer is usually so referred to in the counter-offer as to be no mistaking what it is aimed at.

Article 19 of the United Nations Convention on Contracts for the International Sale of Goods stipulates as follows:

1. A reply to an offer which purports to be an acceptance but contains additions,

limitations or other modifications is a rejection of the offer and constitutes a counter-offer.

2. However, a reply to an offer which purports to be an acceptance but contains additional or different terms which do not materially alter the terms of the offer constitutes an acceptance, unless the offeror, without undue delay, objects orally to the discrepancy or dispatches a notice to that effect. If he does not so object, the terms of the contract are the terms of the offer with the modifications contained in the acceptance.

3. Additional or different terms relating, among other things, to the price, payment, quality and quantity of the goods, place and time of delivery, extent of one party's liability to the other or the settlement of disputes are considered to alter the terms of the offer materially.

Chapter 7　Orders
订货

Learning Objectives

- Understand the definition of an order
- Comprehend the key components of an order form
- Master the main contents involved in an order letter
- Master the skills in writing an order letter

学习目标:理解订单的含义;掌握订单表中的关键内容;掌握订单信涉及的主要内容及写作的技巧。

Case Study

After FG received the counter-offer from Jin Yuan Corp, they found the counter-offer was acceptable. So they would like to place an order with Jin Yuan Corp. What could be included in the order letter?

Introduction

When the buyers or the sellers agree with the terms of an offer, they usually place an order—a formal request for the transaction of certain goods for a specified quantity. An order can be an acceptance of an offer or sent voluntarily by the buyer. It should state clearly and accurately all the terms of transaction including the specification, the price, terms of payment, quality, quantity, time of delivery, port of destination. Normally a Sales Confirmation may be worked out by both parties on the basis of terms and conditions in the order. Thus the deal is concluded.

Sometimes the sellers cannot accept the buyer's order because the goods required are not available or the prices or specifications have been adjusted. Such letters must be written with the utmost care and with an eye to goodwill and future business. Sometimes the seller can recommend suitable substitutes or make counter-offers to persuade the buyers to accept them.

Specimen Letters

样信

Letter 1: Order from FG

Dear Mr. Li,

We have received your e-mail of Jan. 11th, 2025. After due consideration, we have pleasure in **confirming** the following offer:

1. Commodity: mulberry silk textile.
2. Specifications: silk yarn containing 85% or less, and other blended.
3. Package: export standard carton (50 pcs per carton, net weight 4 kg/carton, gross weight 5kg/carton).
4. Quantity: 20,000 pcs in 400 cartons, 50 pcs/carton.
5. Quality: 2024 new product.
6. Price: USD 2.50/pc, CIF Marseille.
7. Payment: L/C at sight which should reach the seller before March 1th, 2025.
8. Shipment: Not later than Apr. 20th, 2025.

Please send us your S/C, and we hope both of us may have a wonderful beginning.

Yours faithfully,

Letter 2: Order with Order Form

Dear Sirs,

Thank you very much for your offer dated Nov. 9th. After careful consideration, we decided to accept your terms and conditions and place a trial order for the four items mentioned in our **attached** Order Form. We will place regular orders with you as long as the quality is up to our expectation.

This order is subject to shipment without delay before Chinese New Year—Spring Festival.

Enclosed please find our Order Form.

We look forward to your early reply.

Yours faithfully,

Encl.

Order No. 123

ORDER FORM

14th November, 2025

Qty	Item	Catalogue No.	CIF Sydney Net
248	Bed Sheets, 120 cm, red	65	US $ 3.5 each
248	Bed Sheets, 105 cm, yellow	98	US $ 4.6 each
356	Pillow Cases, blue	205	US $ 2.6 a pair
356	Pillow Cases, pink	210	US $ 2.6 a pair

Packing: in cotton cloth bales.

Shipment: prompt shipment from Tianjin.

Payment: by **irrevocable L/C** available by draft at sight.

for T. SMITH & CO., LTD

Letter 3: Repeat Order

Dear Sirs,

Re: Spring Women's Blouses 165/92, 170/98

We have received the captioned shipment ex S. S. Peace and are glad to inform you that we find the quality and the price quite satisfactory. In fact, your first shipment of the blouses has been well accepted in our market. As we believe we can sell additional quantities in the market, we want to place a repeat order with you for 3,000 pieces of the same styles and sizes individually.

As all these items are urgently required by our customers, we hope you will make delivery at an early date.

Yours faithfully,

Letter 4: Decline an Order

Dear Sirs,

Thank you for your fax of May 3rd in which you informed us that you wish to place a repeat order with us for our Spring Blouses 165/92, 170/98.

Much as we would like to expand our business with you, we feel regretful that we are not **in a position** to **entertain any fresh orders** for the above-mentioned goods, owing to **heavy commitments.** However, we shall not fail to contact you as soon as we are able to accept new orders.

Regarding our spring blouses, we are enclosing a list for your study in case you are interested in any other items. If possible, please do not hesitate to let us know your detailed requirements.

Yours faithfully,

Encl.

Letter 5: E-mail for a PI for Numan MP4, M6000

To:

Cc:

From:

Subject: Re: PI for Numan MP4, M6000

Dear John,

Very glad to hear that you confirmed the price US $ 52.5/set. I'm writing today to send you the PI for running this order with 200 dozen.

Please check the file with unit price, packaging, delivery time, payment terms, and so on. If no additional questions, please sign back the PI.

As soon as we get your final confirmation, we will arrange for shipment.

Best regards,

Letter 6: Specimen of a Sales Contract

Sales Contract

编号 S/C No.: FG 20250112

日期 Date: JAN. 12, 2025

签约地点 Signed at: BEIJING

卖方 Sellers: JIN YUAN IMPORT AND EXPORT CO., LTD.

地址 Address: No. 118 XUEYUAN ROAD, BEIJING, CHINA

邮政编码 Postal Code: 100081

电话 Tel: 86-10-87160000

传真 Fax: 86-10-87160000

买方 Buyers：FASHION GENERAL TRADING CO.

地 址 Address：15 RUE MARQUISE DU CHATELET，ZONE INDUSTRIELLE FAIRNCERIES，12500，LUNEVILLE，FRANCE

邮政编码 Postal Code：12500

电话 Tel：0033-3-82340000

传真 Fax：0033-3-82340000

买卖双方同意按下列条款由卖方出售，买方购进下列货物：

The Sellers agree to sell and the Buyers agree to buy the under-mentioned goods on the terms and conditions stated below：

1. 名称及规格 Commodity	2. 数量 Quantity	3. 单价 Unit Price	4. 金额 Amount
MULBERRY SILK TEXTILE（SILK YARN CONTAINING 85% OR LESS，AND OTHER BLENDED）	20,000 PCS	USD 2.50/PC CIF MARSEILLE	USD 50,000

5. 总值 Total Amount：SAY U.S. DOLLARS FIFTY THOUSAND ONLY

数量及总值均有 5%的增减，由卖方决定。

With 5% more or less both in amount and quantity allowed at the Seller's option.

6. 生产国和制造厂家 Country of Origin and Manufacture：CHINA

7. 包装 Packing：TO BE PACKED IN EXPORT STANDARD CARTONS OF 50 PCS EACH

8. 唛头 Shipping Marks：FG 20250112

CIF MARSEILLE

FRANCE

9. 装运期限 Time of Shipment：NOT LATER THAN APR. 20，2025

10. 装运口岸 Port of Loading：TIANJIN PORT，CHINA

11. 到达口岸 Port of Destination：MARSEILLE，FRANCE

12. 保险 Insurance：由卖方按发票金额的 110%投保至马赛为止的一切险。

To be covered by the SELLERS for 110% of full invoice value covering ALL RISKS up to MARSEILLE only.

13. 付款条件 Terms of Payment：L/C AT SIGHT FOR 100% OF INVOICE VALUE WHICH SHOULD REACH THE SELLER BEFORE MAR. 1, 2025.

14. 单据 Documents：

(1) SIGNED COMMERCIAL INVOICE IN TWO ORIGINALS INDICATING S/C NO. AND L/C NO.

(2) INSURANCE POLICY IN TWO ORIGINALS TO ORDER OF THE ISSUING BANK IN THE CURRENCY OF THE CREDIT COVERING ALL RISKS OF OCEAN MARINE CARGO CLAUSES FOR 110% INVOICE VALUE.

(3) CERTIFICATE OF ORIGIN SIGNED BY THE BENEFICIARY.

(4) FULL SET CLEAN ON BOARD BILL OF LADING MADE OUT TO ORDER MARKED FREIGHT PREPAID AND NOTIFY APPLICANT, INDICATING THE FULL NAME, ADDRESS AND TEL NO. OF THE CARRYING VESSEL'S AGENT AT THE PORT OF DISCHARGE.

(5) PACKING LIST IN ONE ORIGINAL PLUS ONE COPY, ALL OF WHICH MUST BE MANUALLY SIGNED.

15. 装运条件 Terms of Shipment：THE LATEST DATE APR. 20, 2025, BY VESSEL FROM TIANJIN PORT, CHINA TO MARSEILLE PORT, FRANCE AND TRANSSHIPMENT PROHIBITED, PARTIAL SHIPMENT PROHIBITED.

16. 品质与数量、重量的异议与索赔 Quality/Quantity Discrepancy and Claim：

(1)货物到达目的港口岸后，买方可委托当地的商品检验机构对货物进行复检。如果发现货物有损坏、残缺或规格、数量与合同规定不符，买方凭检验机构出具的检验证明向卖方索赔。

The buyers have the right to have the goods re-inspected by the local commodity inspection authority after the arrival of the goods at the port of destination. If the goods are found damaged/short/their specifications and quantities not in compliance with that specified in the contract, the buyers shall lodge claims against the sellers based on the Inspection Certificate issued by the Commodity Inspection Authority.

(2)如买方提出索赔,凡属品质异议须于货到目的口岸之日起30日内提出;凡属数量异议须于货到目的口岸之日起15日内提出。对货物所提任何异议应由保险公司、运输公司或邮递机构负责的,卖方不负任何责任。

The claims, if any regarding to the quality of the goods, shall be lodged within 30 days after arrival of the goods at the destination; if any regarding to the quantities of the goods, shall be lodged within 15 days after arrival of the goods at the destination. The Sellers shall not take any responsibility if any claim concerning the shipping goods is up to the responsibility of Insurance Company/Transportation Company/Post Office.

17. 不可抗力 Force Majeure:

如因洪水、火灾、地震、干旱、战争或其他人力不可预见、控制、避免或克服的事件造成本合同全部或部分不能履约,任何一方都不需要承担责任。但是,遭受不可抗力事件的一方应立即书面通知另一方该事故的发生情况,并在事故发生后15天内向对方寄出由相关机构出具的事件证明。

Either party shall not be held responsible for failure or delay to perform all or any part of this contract due to flood, fire, earthquake, draught, war or any other events which could not be predicted, controlled, avoided or overcome by the relative party. However, the party affected by the event of Force Majeure shall inform the other party of its occurrence in writing as soon as possible and send a certificate of event issued by the relevant authorities to the other party within 15 days after its occurrence.

18. 仲裁 Arbitration:

凡因执行本合约或有关本合约所发生的一切争执,双方应协商解决。如果协商不能得到解决,应提交中国国际贸易促进委员会对外贸易仲裁委员会依据其程序进行仲裁。仲裁裁决是终局的,对双方都有约束力,仲裁费用由败诉方承担。

All disputes arising from the execution of this contract shall be settled through friendly consultation. In case no settlement can be reached, the case in dispute shall be submitted to the Foreign Trade Arbitration Commission of the China Council for the Promotion of International Trade for arbitration in accordance with its Provisional Rules of Procedure. The decision made by this commission shall be regarded as final and binding upon both parties. Arbitration fees shall be borne by the losing party, unless otherwise awarded.

Buyer: Tony Brown　　Seller: 李亮

Date: Jan. 12, 2025　　Date: Jan. 12, 2025

Words & Phrases 词汇

1. confirm v. 确认,证实,常用在外贸书信的开头,表示证实自己的去信(电)或收到对方的来信(电)

We confirm acceptance of your order.

我们确认接受贵方订单。

We hereby confirm having sold you 2,000 sets of air conditioners on the terms and conditions specified below.

我们兹确认向贵方出售 2 000 台空调,条款如下。

confirmation n. 确认,证实

We offer you as follows subject to our final confirmation.

我方向贵方报盘如下,以我方最后确认为准。

We thank you for your immediate confirmation of our order.

感谢贵方对我们订单的立即确认。

2. attached a. 随附的

The brochure attached will give you details of the items we can supply at present.

随附的小册子将给出当前我们所能供货的商品的详细资料。

3. irrevocable L/C 不可撤销的信用证

revocable L/C 可撤销的信用证

4. much as... 虽然很……

Much as we would like to come to terms with you, we cannot entertain your counter-offer.

虽然我们很想与贵方达成交易,但我们不能接受贵方的还盘。

Much as we are interested in your products, we cannot place an order with you because of the high price.

虽然我们对贵方的产品很感兴趣,但因为价格太高,我们不能向贵方订货。

5. be in a position to 能够

If you are in a position to meet our demand, we will place repeat orders for this article.

如果贵方能同意我们的要求,我们将对该货物续订货。

6. entertain any fresh orders 接受任何新订单

entertain v. 考虑(引申为准备接受)

We are too heavily committed to be able to entertain any fresh orders.

我方任务太重了,不能考虑任何新订单。

They would not entertain any price higher than US $ 400 per metric ton.

他们将不考虑任何高于每公吨400美金的价格。

We shall be glad to entertain any constructive suggestion you may make.

我方将乐于考虑贵方可能提出的任何建设性的建议。

7. heavy commitment 任务过重,承诺过多

commitment n. 允诺,承诺

As far as our information goes, the company punctually meets its commitments.

就我们所知,该公司准时守信。

Heavy commitments prevent us from accepting new orders.

过多的订单使我们无法接受新的订单。

8. PI, proforma invoice 形式发票

Useful Sentences 常用句型

1. If you can execute the order to our full satisfaction, we will place further orders with you.

如果贵方订单的执行可以令我们完全满意,我们将向贵方更多的订货。

2. Thank you for your offer of March 4th. Your prices and quality are satisfactory

and we are sending you an order as follows.

感谢贵方3月4日的报盘。贵方的价格和质量都是令人满意的,我们发给贵方一份订单,内容如下。

3. We appreciate your cooperation and trust that your order goods will turn out to your full satisfaction.

我们感谢贵方的合作,相信贵方订单之商品会让贵方完全满意。

4. We intend to place with you a repeat order for 2,000 men's shirt of the same style and sizes.

我们打算与贵方续订同样式样和尺码的2 000件男式衬衫。

5. We place the order on the condition that the goods are dispatched in time to reach us by April 3rd. We would like to remind you that we reserve the right to cancel it and to refuse to take delivery after the date.

我们向贵方订货,要求货物及时发运以便在4月3日前到达我方。我们想提醒贵方,对于此日期后的交货,我们将保留取消订单并拒绝提货的权利。

6. We thank you very much for your initial order and hope that this may be the beginning of the long and friendly relations between us.

非常感谢贵方的首次订货,希望这是我们之间长期友好关系的开始。

7. We have cut our price to the limit. We regret, therefore, being unable to comply with your request for further reduction.

我们已将价格降至最低限度,所以很遗憾我们不能满足贵方提出的进一步降价的要求。

8. Your order is receiving our immediate attention, and you can depend on us to make delivery well within your time limit.

贵方订单受到我们的密切关注,请相信我们会在贵方规定的时间内交货。

9. With reference to your letter of September 5th, we have pleasure in informing you that we have booked your order for 2,000 sets of air conditioners. We are sending you our S/C No. 387 in duplicate, one copy of which please sign and return for our file.

按照贵方9月5日来函,我们很高兴地通知贵方,我们接受贵方2 000台空调的订单。我们现给贵方发送我们的第387号售货确认书,一式两份,请签字并退还一份以便我们存档。

10. We trust this initial order will lead to further dealings between our two companies.

我们相信首份订单将会给我们两家公司带来更多的交易。

11. As this is your initial order, we have decided to grant you 3% special discount to strengthen your position in competition with other suppliers.

由于这是贵方的首份订单,我们决定给予贵方 3%的特别折扣以巩固贵方在与其他供应商竞争中的地位。

12. All these items are urgently required by our customers, we, therefore, hope you will make delivery at an early date.

所有这些商品都是我们客户急需的,因此,我们希望贵方能尽早交货。

13. We have substituted material No. 21 for No. 23, as the latter is not available at present.

我们已经用第 21 号材质取代 23 号材质,因为后者目前不可供。

14. We feel sure you will find our goods satisfactory in every way and perfectly suitable for your needs.

我们相信贵方会发现我们的产品在各方面都是令人满意的,并能完全满足贵方的需要。

Exercises 练习

Ⅰ. Translate the following sentences into Chinese.

1. If your prices compare favorably to those of other suppliers, we shall send you an order.

2. Your order is receiving our immediate attention and you can depend on us to make delivery well within your time limit.

3. We hope the goods will reach you in good time and look forward to receiving your further orders.

4. As our customers are urgently in need of these goods, we hope you will send them at an early date.

5. We confirm 10,000 dozen of tablecloths at the prices stated in your letter and will arrange for delivery by the first available steamer upon receipt of your L/C.

6. We thank you for this order, and hope we may have the pleasure of supplying

you again in the near future.

7. We must insist on immediate delivery, otherwise, we shall be compelled to cancel the order in accordance with the contract stipulations.

8. We find both quality and prices satisfactory and are pleased to give you a repeat order for the following items on the understanding that they will be supplied from stock at the prices stated.

9. If the article needed is out of stock, please substitute it with a similar one.

10. We expect to find a good market for the above and hope to place further and larger orders with you in the near future.

Ⅱ. Translate the following sentences into English.

1. 请放心,我们将按照双方商定的条件执行贵方订单。

2. 因为存货售罄,我方不能接受新订单。但是一俟新货源到来,我方即去电与贵方联系。

3. 我方要强调的是,此次是我方首次向贵方订购,如首批交货令人满意,我方将续订并长期订购。

4. 如贵方对这些商品有兴趣,我们能够报价,货物数量有限,4 月份发货。

5. 如贵方立即订购,我方可在本月装运。

6. 请从速办理订单,不胜感激。

7. 请按照贵公司提供的样品供应我公司 50 公吨苦杏仁。

8. 非常遗憾地通知贵公司,因为购货人对贵公司价格不予确认,因此我们不得不取消此订单。

9. 贵方报盘中的价格及质量都令我方满意,现随附如下订单。

10. 我们预计这批货会很畅销,并希望不久能再次向贵公司下更大的订单。

Ⅲ. Fill in the contract forms in English with the particulars from the following messages.

Sellers: Beijing Light Industrial Products Imp & Exp Corp.

Buyers: Boston Trading Co., Ltd.

(1) Please quote your lowest price for 1,000 dozen fountain pens Model LC001

CFR Boston.

(2) As requested, we are making you a firm offer as follows:

1,000 dozen fountain pens, Model LC001, packed in boxes of one dozen each and 20 boxes to a carton, at US $ 20 per dozen CFR Boston for shipment during March/April 2025. Payment is to be made by confirmed, irrevocable L/C payable by draft at sight.

(3) While we thank you for the above offer, we regret to say that your price is too high to be acceptable. There is no possibility of this deal unless you reduce your price by 5%.

(4) In view of our long business relations, we accept your counter-offer. Please send us your order by return.

(5) We are pleased to confirm having ordered 1,000 dozen fountain pens on the terms and conditions stated in our counter-offer. Please send us the relevant S/C.

(6) Enclosed is our S/C No. 5454 signed in Beijing on 18th January, 2025.

Contract No.

Sellers:

Buyers:

This Contract is made by and between the Buyers and the Sellers, whereby the Buyers agree to buy and the Sellers agree to sell the under-mentioned commodity according to the terms and conditions stipulated below:

Commodity:

Specifications:

Quantity:

Unit Price:

Total Value:

Packing:

Shipping Mark:

Insurance:

Time of Shipment:

Port of Shipment:

Port of Destination:

Terms of Payment:

Done and signed in on this day of , .

Ⅳ. Translate the following letter into Chinese.

Dear Sirs,

"Parrot" Brand White Cement

As a result of our recent exchange of telegrams, we confirm having purchased from you for 1,000 long tons of the captioned goods on the following terms and conditions:

Price: At €225 per long ton CFR Genoa, net shipping weight

Packing: In 6-ply craft-paper bags of about 110 lbs net each

Quality: Against the Seller's own guarantee that the goods are fully up to the Chinese Export Standard

Shipment: In one or two lots to be shipped from Qinhuangdao to Genoa during January, 2025, preferably by direct steamer

Payment: By a confirmed and irrevocable letter of credit in your favor, available by draft at sight

We are pleased to have transacted this first business with your corporation and look forward to the further expansion of trade to our mutual benefit.

Yours faithfully,

Ⅴ. Translate the following letter into English.

敬启者:

事由:第78PG017号合同

我们已经收到通过"东风"号装运的标题项的商品。我们很高兴地告知贵方我们认为商品是令人满意的。由于我们认为可以在该市场销售更多的数量,我们打算做一个重复订单,相同样式和尺寸,数量为1 000打。如果可能,请尽早安排装运,因为我们急需此货。

万一所述货物没有存货,如果贵方能告知我们可供现货的商品规格和详细信息，我们将不胜感激。

谨上

Ⅵ. Letter writing.

Suppose you have received your customer's initial order for wool underwear. Now you are required to reply to it. In your letter, the following particulars should be included: ask the customer to countersign your S/C and return one copy; ensure the order will be executed to the customer's satisfaction; hope for further orders.

Further Reading
扩展阅读

Letter 7: Decline an Order

Dear Sirs,

We thank you for your Order No. 789 but regret very much that we are not in a position to accept it on account of unavailability of raw materials.

We will, however, revert to this matter and contact you as soon as the supply position improves.

Meanwhile, please do not hesitate to send us your enquiries for our other products and we assure you of our prompt attention at all times.

Yours faithfully,

Letter 8: Confirm an Order

Dear Sirs,

We are pleased to receive your order of 3rd October for tablecloths and you are welcome as one of our customers.

We confirm supplying 10,000 dozen of tablecloths at the prices stated in your letter and will arrange for delivery by the first available steamer upon receipt of your L/C. We feel confident that the goods will prove to your complete satisfaction when they reach you.

The contract is being drawn up and will be forwarded to you for countersignature as soon as it is ready. We hope the conclusion of this deal will pave the way for further friendly cooperation between us and mark the beginning of the good relationship.

Yours faithfully,

Letter 9: Refuse an Order

Dear Sirs,

We were very glad to receive your order of November 2nd for 100 Changhong color TV but, since you make delivery before Christmas a firm condition, we deeply regret that we cannot accept it as we have done on so many occasions in the past.

The manufacturers are finding it impossible to meet the current demand for this very popular set. We ourselves placed an order for twenty-four a month ago, but were informed that all offers are being met in strict rotation and that our own could not be dealt with until the beginning of February.

We suppose from our telephone conversation this morning that your customers are unwilling to consider other makes. We hope therefore you will be able to obtain your needs from other sources. May we suggest that you try the Television Service Association. This is the only suggestion we can make. We hope you will find it to be of some use.

Yours sincerely,

Tips

Conclusion of Contract

A contract is an agreement that creates an obligation. It is binding and legally enforceable between two or more competent parties. It generally consists of an exchange of promises—an offer and an acceptance—resulting in an obligation to perform some particular act. In order to be valid, a contract must have the genuine assent of parties to it, that is, it must involve both offer and acceptance. Two important areas of the contract are trade terms and payment terms.

When both parties are arranging an international sales contract, it is important to ensure that there is no confusion over who is responsible for delivering the goods and paying for the transport. Confusion will only lead to delays, loss of profit and create unnecessary problems between you and your trading partner. As an exporter you should use "Incoterms 2020" in your contract to ensure that all the obligations are understood. Incoterms 2020 is a set of rules covering delivery, risks and costs. The rules were developed by the International Chamber of Commerce (ICC) and are recognized in most countries, although do not take precedence over national laws.

Terms of payment should not be confused with Incoterms. Incoterms relates solely to the terms of delivery for the buyer and seller. The terms of payment define the conditions under which the importer and exporter have agreed to settle the financial amount of the sales contract. The basic points include method of payment, date of payment, place of payment, method of remittance, and cost related to the payment.

In keeping with the regular practices in international trade, a written contract or confirmation should be prepared in duplicate: each copy should be signed by both parties, and each party should keep a signed copy of it. Some of the contracts or confirmations commonly used in foreign trade are available in printed form, so that only the date, price, name of commodities, name of parties, and similar particulars need be filed in. A contract can be worked out either by the seller or the buyer, and is called a sales contract or a purchase contract respectively. The same is also applicable to a sales confirmation or a purchase confirmation.

Legally, both the sales contract and the sales confirmation are equally binding on the parties. On the whole, the former is more formal, and the latter, less formal. Besides, the former consists of not only such main terms as the name of commodities, specifications, quantity, packing, marking, price, shipment, port of shipment and port of destination, and payment, but also those clauses concerning insurance, commodity inspection, claims, arbitration and force majeure; while the latter covers several main items only.

Chapter 8 Terms of Payment
支付方式

Learning Objectives

- Master some commonly accepted terms of payment in international trade
- Master the procedures adopted in payment by L/C
- Master the procedures adopted in payment by collection and remittance
- Grasp the steps in writing letters on payment terms
- Grasp the steps in writing letters on amending an L/C

学习目标:了解国际贸易中常用的几种付款方式;理解信用证付款流程;理解托收和汇付的流程;掌握付款类信件的写作步骤;掌握信用证修改信件的写作方法。

Case Study

Jin Yuan signed the contract with FG two months ago. According to their contract, the payment should be made by letter of credit. But up till now, Jin Yuan hadn't received the concerned L/C opened by FG. What should Jinyuan do?

Introduction

Compared with payment for domestic transactions, payment for international trade is more complicated and involves more risks. It should be handled with special care.

Normally three methods of payment are involved in international trade: remittance, collection and letter of credit.

Remittance is often used for down payment, payment of commission, payment for sample, or settlement of claim. It is seldom used for payment in large amount as it involves even greater risks than payment by collection and L/C. T/T (telegraphic transfer) is now the popular form of remittance for its efficiency and convenience.

Payment by collection is usually adopted for long-term business partners or the products with slow sale. There are two types of collection: D/P (documents against payment) and D/A (documents against acceptance). D/P can be at sight or after sight. D/P at sight calls for immediate payment by the buyer to obtain the shipping documents. D/P after sight allows the buyer a certain period of time to make payment before he obtains the shipping documents. D/A allows the buyers to obtain the shipping documents just by offering the acceptance of the draft drawn on him. The bank in payment by collection is not responsible for non-payment of the buyer.

Payment by L/C is the most frequently used method of payment in international trade because it facilitates the sellers and the buyers. L/C is a written undertaking by the issuing bank (the agent for the importer) to the beneficiary (the exporter), under which the bank undertakes to pay the beneficiary within the designated time against the stipulated terms and documents.

Remittance and collection are both terms of payment based on commercial credit, while L/C is based on the bank credit.

Specimen Letters

样信

Letter 1: Urging Establishment of a Letter of Credit

Dear Sirs,

Re: Our Sales Confirmation No. FG 20250112

With reference to the 20,000 pieces of mulberry silk textile under our Sales Confirmation No. 20250112, we wish to draw your attention to the fact that the date of delivery is approaching, but we have not yet received your **covering** letter of credit to date. Please do your utmost to **expedite the same**, so that we may **execute the contract** smoothly.

In order to avoid subsequent **amendments**, please **see to it that** the L/C **stipulations should be in exact accordance with** the terms of the Contract.

We hope to receive advice of the L/C soon.

Yours faithfully,

Letter 2: Applying for a Letter of Credit

Dear Sirs,

We enclose an application form for **documentary credit** and shall be glad if you will arrange to **open for our account** an irrevocable letter of credit for USD 50,000.00 **in favor of** Jin Yuan Import and Export Co., LTD., the credit to be valid until May 5, 2025.

The credit which **evidences** shipment of 20,000 pieces of mulberry may be used against **presentation** of the following documents: Bills of Lading **in triplicate**, Certificate of Insurance, two copies each of Signed Invoice, Signed Packing List, and Certificate of Origin. The company may **draw on you at 30 days** for each shipment.

Yours sincerely,

Encl.

Letter 3: Bank Agrees to Open a Letter of Credit

Dear Sirs,

As instructed in your letter of Jan. 28, 2025, we are **issuing** the letter of credit in favor of Jin Yuan Import and Export Co., LTD., valid until May 5, 2025.

Please check the enclosed credit to ensure that it agrees with your instructions. As soon as the credit is **honored**, we shall **debit your account** with us for the amount to be drawn against the L/C.

You can **rest assured** that we will carefully carry out your instructions.

Yours sincerely,

Encl.

A LETTER OF CREDIT

SEQUENCE OF TOTAL	27:1/1	
FORM OF DOCUMENTARY CREDIT	40 A:	IRREVOCABLE

DOCUMENTARY CREDIT NUMBER	20: LC00123756
DATE OF ISSUE	31 C: 2025/03/01
APPLICABLE RULES	40 E: UCP600
DATE AND PLACE OF EXPIRY	31D: DATE 250411, PLACE FRANCE
APPLICANT BANK	51 A: BNP Paribas
APPLICANT	50: FASHION GENERAL TRADING CO. 15 RUE MARQUISE DU CHATELET, ZONE INDUSTRIELLE FAIRNCERIES, 12500, LUNEVILLE, FRANCE Tel: 0033-3-82340000 Fax: 0033-3-82340000
BENEFICIARY	59: JINYUAN IMPORT AND EXPORT CO., LTD. No. 118 XUEYUAN ROAD, BEIJING, CHINA Tel: 86-10-87160000 Fax: 86-10-87160000
CURRENCY CODE, AMOUNT	32 B: CURRENCY USD AMOUNT 50,000.00
AVAILABLE WITH .../BY...	41 D: ANY BANK IN CHINA, BY NEGOTIATION
DRAFTS AT...	42 C: AT 60 DAYS AFTER SIGHT
DRAWEE	42 A: BNP Paribas CORPORATION Paribas HEAD OFFICE
PARTIAL SHIPMENTS	43 P: NOT ALLOWED
TRANSSHIPMENT	43 T: NOT ALLOWED
LOADING ON BOARD/DISPATCH /TAKING IN CHARGE AT/FROM	44 A: CHINA MAIN PORT
FOR TRANSPORTATION TO...	44 B: MARSEILLE PORT, FRANCE
LATEST DATE OF SHIPMENT	44 C: 250420
DESCRIPTION OF GOODS	45 A: MULBERRY SILK TEXTILE (SILK YARN CONTAINING 85% OR LESS, AND OTHER BLENDED)
DOCUMENTS REQUIRED	46 A:

+ SIGNED COMMERCIAL INVOICE IN 2 ORIGINALS INDICATING S/C NO.

FG20250112 AND L/C NO.
+ FULL SET CLEAN ON BOARD BILL OF LADING MADE OUT TO ORDER MARKED FREIGHT PREPAID AND NOTIFY APPLICANT, INDICATING THE FULL NAME, ADDRESS AND TEL NO. OF THE CARRYING VESSEL'S AGENT AT THE PORT OF DISCHARGE.
+ PACKING LIST IN 1 ORIGINAL PLUS 1 COPY, ALL OF WHICH MUST BE MANUALLY SIGNED.
+ CERTIFICATE OF ORIGIN SIGNED BY THE BENEFICIARY.
INSURANCE POLICY IN 2 ORIGINALS TO ORDER OF THE ISSUING BANK IN THE CURRENCY OF THIS CREDIT COVERING ALL RISKS OF OCEAN MARINE CARGO CLAUSES FOR 110% INVOICE VALUE.
ADDITIONAL CONDITIONS 47 A: A DISCREPANCY FEE OF USD 50.00 WILL BE IMPOSED ON EACH SET OF DOCUMENTS PRESENTED FOR NEGOTIATION UNDER THIS L/C WITH DISCREPANCY. THE FEE WILL BE DEDUCTED FROM THE BILL AMOUNT.
CHARGES 71 B: ALL CHARGES AND COMMISSIONS OUTSIDE FRANCE ARE FOR ACCOUNT OF BENEFICIARY.
PERIOD FOR PRESENTATION 48: DOCUMENTS SHOULD BE PRESENTED FOR NEGOTIATIONS WITHIN 21 DAYS AFTER THE DATE OF SHIPMENT BUT WITHIN THE VALIDITY OF THIS CREDIT.
CONFIRMATION INSTRUCTIONS 49: WITHOUT
INSTRUCTION TO THE PAYING/ 78: DOCUMENTS TO BE ACCEPTING/NEGOTIATING BANK DISPATCHED IN ONE LOT BY COURIER TO BNP Paribas (HEAD OFFICE)
SENDER TO RECEIVER INFORMATION 72: REIMBURSEMENT IS SUBJECT TO ICC URR 525

Letter 4: Advise of Letter of Credit

ORIGINAL

Megabank Corporation

OUR ADVICE NUMBER: EA0000091

ADVICE DATE: 08, MAR. 2025 | AMOUNT

ISSUE BANK REF: BPN 2222221 | USD 50,000

EXPIRY DATE: 11, MAY. 2025

BENEFICIARY:

JINYUAN IMPORT AND EXPORT CO., LTD.

No. 118 XUEYUAN ROAD, BEIJING, CHINA

Tel: 86-10-87160000　　Fax: 86-10-87160000

APPLICANT:

FASHION GENERAL TRADING CO.

15 RUE MARQUISE DU CHATELET,

ZONE INDUSTRIELLE FAIRNCERIES

12500, LUNEVILLE, FRANCE

Tel: 0033-3-82340000　　Fax: 0033-3-82340000

WE HAVE BEEN REQUESTED TO ADVISE TO YOU THE FOLLOWING LETTER OF CREDIT AS ISSUED BY: BNP PARIBAS (HEAD OFFICE)

PLEASE BE GUIDED BY ITS TERMS AND CONDITIONS AND BY THE FOLLOWING:

CREDIT IS AVAILABLE BY NEGOTIATION OF YOUR DRAFT(S) IN DUPLICATE AT SIGHT FOR 100 PERCENT OF INVOICE VALUE DRAWN ON US ACCOMPANIED BY THE FOLLOWING DOCUMENTS:

1. SIGNED COMMERCIAL INVOICE IN 2 ORIGINALS INDICATING S/C NO. FG20250112 AND L/C NO.

2. FULL SET CLEAN ON BOARD BILL OF LADING MADE OUT TO ORDER MARKED FREIGHT PREPAID AND NOTIFY APPLICANT, INDICATING THE FULL NAME, ADDRESS AND TEL NO. OF THE CARRYING VESSEL'S AGENT AT THE PORT OF DISCHARGE.

3. PACKING LIST IN 1 ORIGINAL PLUS 1 COPY, ALL OF WHICH MUST BE MANUALLY SIGNED.

4. CERTIFICATE OF ORIGIN SIGNED BY THE BENEFICIARY.

5. INSURANCE POLICY IN 2 ORIGINALS TO ORDER OF THE ISSUING BANK IN THE CURRENCY OF THIS CREDIT COVERING ALL RISKS OF OCEAN MARINE CARGO CLAUSES FOR 110% INVOICE VALUE.

EVIDENCING SHIPMENT OF: MULBERRY SILK TEXTILE (SILK YARN CONTAINING 85% OR LESS, AND OTHER BLENDED)

SHIPMENT FROM: CHINA MAIN PORT TO: MARSEILLE PORT, FRANCE

LATEST SHIPPING DATE: 250420

PARTIAL SHIPMENTS NOT ALLOWED TRANSSHIPMENT NOT ALLOWED

ALL BANKING CHARGES OUTSIDE FRANCE ARE FOR ACCOUNT OF BENEFICIARY.

DOCUMENTS MUST BE PRESENTED WITHIN 21 DAYS FROM B/L DATE.

AT THE REQUEST OF OUR CORRESPONDENT, WE CONFIRM THIS CREDIT AND ALSO ENGAGE WITH YOU THAT ALL DRAFTS DRAWN UNDER AND IN COMPLIANCE WITH THE TERMS OF THIS CREDIT WILL BE DULY HONORED BY US.

PLEASE EXAMINE THIS INSTRUMENT CAREFULLY. IF YOU ARE UNABLE TO COMPLY WITH THE TERMS OR CONDITIONS, PLEASE COMMUNICATE WITH YOUR BUYER TO ARRANGE FOR AN AMENDMENT.

Letter 5: Exporter Requests Amendment to L/C

Dear Sirs,

Re: Letter of Credit No. LC00123756

We thank you for your L/C No. LC00123756 covering your order for mulberry silk textile. After having checked the L/C carefully, we find some discrepancies and request you to amend the L/C as follows:

As per the contract, the expiry date and place of L/C should be on May 11, 2025 in China. However, according to the L/C, same is on Apr. 11, 2025 in France. As it is hard for us to negotiate the documents in France, please amend the L/C as per the contract.

As to the payment terms, payment should be made by L/C at sight instead of by L/C 60 days after sight.

Please confirm the amendments as the above by fax, so that we may arrange shipment accordingly.

Yours sincerely,

Letter 6: E-mail for Payment Terms for New Order

To:

Cc:

From:

Subject: Payment terms for new order

Dear John,

We have a proposal for changing the present payment terms. As L/C handling charge is too expensive to our expectation, maybe we could adopt T/T or D/P at sight from the next order. Our top management all agree to alter payment terms for current and future orders. Please notify me of your opinion.

Thanks and best regards,

Words & Phrases 词汇

1. covering a. 有关的,涉及……的,包括……的

The subject cargo will be ready for shipment in a few days and we are looking forward to your covering L/C.

标题项下的货物几天后将备妥待运,我们期待收到贵方相关的信用证。

Please let us have your pricelist covering your typewriters.

请给我们有关贵方打字机的价目单。

covered a. 由……所包含,在……项下

We have shipped on board S. S. "Daqing" 2,500 pairs of rubber shoes covered by your L/C No. 335.

贵方第335号信用证项下的2 500双胶鞋已装"大庆"号。

2. expedite v. 加速

We shall appreciate it if you can expedite shipment as soon as possible.

如果贵方能尽可能快地加速装运,我们将不胜感激。

Please do your utmost to expedite the covering L/C so that we may execute the order smoothly.

请尽力速开相关的信用证以便我们能顺利地执行订单。

3. the same 前面所提的"L/C"

4. execute the contract 执行合同

Please do your utmost to execute this order as it will lead to other business.

请尽力执行该订单,因为它会影响其他交易。

execution n. 执行,实行,签署

We assure you of the punctual execution of your order.

我们向贵方保证按时执行贵方订单。

Party A shall, within 30 days of the execution of this agreement, provide Party B with the list mentioned below.

A方应在执行合同的30天内向B方提供下列明细单。

5. amendment n. 修改,修改书 make amendments

amendment advice, advice of amendment 修改通知书

Please rush the amendment to the L/C.

请加速修改信用证。

We enclose amendment advice of L/C No. 40.

随附第 40 号信用证的修改通知书。

The wording of the agreement calls for amendment.

协议书的措辞需要修改。

amend v. 修改+不定式或 as

Please amend the credit as allowing transshipment.

请修改信用证,允许转运。

Please amend the amount of the L/C to read "2% more or less".

请将信用证金额修改为"2%的增减"。

The amount of the L/C has been amended as US $ 6,000.

信用证的金额已被修改为 6 000 美金。

6. see to it... 要注意使……, 务必使……, 保证使……

Please see to it that the L/C should be established as per the relevant contract.

请注意信用证应按照相关合同开立。

Please see to it that the L/C should reach here before the end of this month.

请注意信用证应在本月底前开到此地。

7. stipulation n. 规定,条款(适用于合同、信用证等),项目

The transaction is concluded on the stipulations that L/C should be opened 30 days before the commencement of shipment.

按照达成交易的条款,信用证应在装运前 30 天开立。

The transaction is settled down with the stipulation of direct shipment.

交易规定直达运输。

stipulate v. 规定

We regret to find that the goods were not packed as stipulated.

我们很遗憾地发现货物未按规定包装。

The contract stipulates payment by sight L/C.

合同规定付款方式为即期信用证。

The contract stipulates that the goods (should) be shipped entire.

合同规定货物必须一次全部装运。

8. be in exact accordance with... 与……完全一致

in strict/full/precise accordance with 与……严格一致

The letter of credit established should be in exact accordance with the Sales Contract.

所开立的信用证应与销售合同完全一致。

9. documentary credit 跟单信用证

有关信用证的部分常见短语:confirmed L/C 保兑信用证,irrevocable L/C 不可撤销信用证,transferable and divisible L/C 可转让与可分割信用证,revolving L/C 循环信用证,back to back L/C 背对背信用证,reciprocal L/C 对开信用证

10. open v. 开(证)

open/establish/issue an L/C 开证。其中普通的表述是 open an L/C,比较正式的表述是 establish an L/C,从银行角度表述为 issue an L/C。

Letter of credit will be opened (established) in a few days.

信用证近日内即开。

We have arranged with our bankers to issue an L/C in your favor.

我们已安排我方银行向贵方开出信用证。

11. for our account 由我方负担,以我方为开证申请人

(to be)for sb.'s account, for the account of 由某人负担

The arbitration fees shall be for the account of the losing party.

仲裁费由败诉方承担。

12. in favor of... 以……为受益人

The letter of credit has been opened in your favor.

信用证以贵方为受益人开立。

13. evidence v. 证明 n. 证据,根据

The intact packing evidenced that the goods were damaged before shipment.

完整的包装证明货物是在装运前受损的。

There was not enough evidence to prove that the goods were damaged before shipment.

无足够的证据证明货物是在装运前受损的。

14. presentation n. 提交,出示,提供

On D/A terms, all drafts must be accepted by the drawee upon presentation.

在承兑交单付款方式下,所有的汇票在提示时必须由见票人承兑。

15. in triplicate 一式三份

in duplicate 一式两份, in quadruplicate/in four copies/in four fold 一式四份

Applications must be made out in triplicate.

申请书必须填写一式三份。

16. draw on sb. at 30 days, draw a draft on sb. at 30 days 给某人开立 30 天的汇票

We have drawn a clean draft on you for the balance of US $90.

我们就 90 美金的余额给贵方开出一张光票。

drawer 汇票的出票人,drawee 汇票的见票人

17. honor v. 承兑,付款

Please honor our draft when they are presented to you by our bankers.

当我方银行向贵方提示我们所开立的汇票时,请付款。

18. debit your account with the amount 借记贵方账户

debit v. 把……记入借方 n. 借记,记入借方的款项

debit an amount to sb.'s account/debit one's account with an amount 借记某人的账户一笔金额

His account with the bank has been debited with the sum of US $2 for half-yearly bank charges.

他的银行账户被借记 2 美金,以支付银行半年的费用。

to the debit of one's account 记入某人账户的借方

19. rest assured 请放心

rest assured/be assured 放心

Please rest assured (You may rest assured) that we shall try our best to deliver the goods by end May.

请放心我们将尽力 5 月底前交货。

You may be assured of our regular supply of walnuts.

请放心我们会定期供应核桃。

Useful Sentences 常用句型

1. Our usual terms of payment are made by confirmed, irrevocable letter of credit in our favor, available by draft at sight, reaching us one month ahead of shipment, remaining valid for negotiation in China for 21 days after the prescribed time of shipment.

我们通常的付款方式是保兑的、不可撤销的、以我方为受益人的信用证,凭即期汇票使用,装运前一个月到达我方,在规定的装船时间后 21 天内在中国议付有效。

2. In compliance with your request, we will make an exception to our rules and accept delivery against D/P at 30 days, but this should not be regarded as a precedent.

按照贵方的要求,我们破例接受 30 天的付款交单方式,但这不应该被视为一个先例。

3. It would be advisable for you to establish the covering letter of credit as early as possible so as to enable us to arrange shipment in due time.

贵方最好尽早开立相关的信用证以便我们能够在适当的时间安排装运。

4. We are unable to effect shipment according to the price and other terms originally agreed upon owing to the delay of your letter of credit, and therefore the responsibility for any loss arising subsequently will wholly rest with you.

由于贵方信用证开立的延误,我们无法按照原先达成的价格和其他条款安排装运,因此所产生的任何损失的责任将完全由贵方承担。

5. We regret our inability to make any arrangement contrary to our usual practice, which is payment by confirmed, irrevocable letter of credit payable against presentation of shipping documents and valid for at least 15 days beyond the promised date of shipment.

很遗憾我们无法做出任何与我们通常做法不一致的安排,我们通常的做法是保兑的、不可撤销的、凭提交装运单据来使用的信用证,有效期限和约定的装运时间至少相隔 15 天。

6. As regards L/C No. 422, please extend by fax the shipment date to Mar. 15 and expiry date to Mar. 30.

关于第 422 号信用证，请用传真将其装运日期延长为 3 月 15 日，信用证有效期延长至 3 月 30 日。

7. Considering the long business relationship between us, we agree to change the terms of payment from L/C to D/P.

鉴于我们之间长期的业务关系，我们同意将付款方式由信用证付款变更为付款交单方式。

8. In view of the amount of this transaction being very small, we are prepared to accept payment by D/P at 60 days after sight for the value of the goods shipped.

考虑到交易金额不大，我们准备接受 60 天的付款交单方式，金额为货物价值。

9. Please amend L/C No. 432 allowing transshipment and partial shipment, so that we may effect shipment without delay.

请修改第 432 号信用证，允许转船和分批装运，以便我们能立即装运。

10. We have surrendered to the Bank of China, Fuzhou, clean shipped on board Bs/L in complete set together with other documents according to the terms of your L/C No. 322.

根据第 322 号信用证我们已经向位于福州的中国银行提交整套清洁已装船提单以及其他单据。

11. We agree to accept the above mentioned draft on presentation, and pay the amount thereof at maturity, provided such draft shall be negotiated within three months from this date.

只要汇票自今日起三个月内议付，我们同意该汇票在被提示时承兑，到期付款。

12. As there is no direct sailing from Yantai to London, please delete the clause "by direct vessel" and insert the wording "transshipment is allowed".

由于从烟台到伦敦没有直达航班，请删除"通过直达船"条款，加上"允许转船"。

13. The amendment advice should reach us by the end of this month, failing which you must extend the validity of the L/C to April 15.

修改通知书应该本月底前到达我方，否则贵方必须将信用证的有效期限延长到 4 月 15 日。

Exercises 练习

Ⅰ. Translate the following sentences into Chinese.

1. With reference to the goods under our Sales Confirmation No. 3232, we wish to draw your attention to the fact that the date of delivery is approaching, but we have not yet received the covering L/C to date.

2. We are prepared to accept payment for your trial order on D/P basis.

3. We regret that we are unable to consider your request for payment under D/A terms.

4. The original shipping documents have been presented to the confirming bank here for payment.

5. In order to avoid subsequent amendments, please see to it that the stipulations in the L/C are in exact accordance with the terms of the contract.

6. The letter of credit authorizes you to draw at 60 days' on the bank in New York for the amount of your invoice after shipment is made.

7. Since there is no further reason to delay payment, we expect your fax confirmation of acceptance of our 60 days' draft drawn on you.

8. We are looking forward to receiving your bank's extension of the above L/C thus enabling us to effect shipment of the goods in question.

9. Draft must be accompanied by a full set of original clean on board marine Bills of Lading made out to order, endorsed in blank, marked "freight prepaid".

10. We appreciate your cooperation in quotation, but we also advise you to make some adjustments to your terms of payment.

Ⅱ. Translate the following sentences into English.

1. 根据贵方要求,我们将破例同意 30 天的承兑交单付款方式。

2. 如同意在支付方面做出让步,如即期付款交单,我们将不胜感激。

3. 请贵方将信用证做如下修改:"吨"前删去"长"字,加入"公"字。

4. 贵方必须从速开证,否则,我们就不能在本月底以前装船。

5. 贵方须在 2025 年 3 月 2 日前开出信用证,否则我方保留撤销合同的权利,不另行通知。

6. 很遗憾地通知贵方,我们的贸易惯例是不接受承兑交单的付款条件。

7. 请注意,付款是以保兑的、不可撤销的、允许部分装运和转船、见票即付的信用证支付。

8. 从贵方电传知悉信用证已开,但很遗憾,我方尚未接到银行通知。请敦促伦敦保兑行尽快通知。

9. 根据合约规定,付款方式应为即期信用证,而不是即期付款交单。

10. 贵方衬衣的价格可接受,若同意付款交单的付款条件,拟试订购2 000 件。

Ⅲ. Translate the following letter into Chinese.

Dear Sirs,

We acknowledge receipt of your Sales Confirmation No. AS05 with great pleasure. We have countersigned it and returned one copy for your file as requested.

In the meantime, as your usual terms of payment are by sight L/C, we have instructed our bank, the National Bank of Dubai Ltd., Cairo Branch, to open the relevant L/C for EURO 600,000 in your favor, which will reach your end soon.

Please pay your best attention to the quality of the goods, the delivery time as well as other terms specified in this S/C. If your execution of this order turns out to be satisfactory, regular orders will be placed in the near future.

Yours faithfully,

Ⅳ. Translate the following letter into English.

敬启者:

我方想告知贵方,贵方第 788 号订单项下的货物已备妥待运相当长时间,但至今我方既没有收到贵方的信用证,也没有收到信函。就此事我方前天给贵方去过电报,但还是没有回复。

如贵方所知,此地每月仅有一艘船舶开往你港,而本月开航的那艘船舱位预定的截止期早过了。因此,对我们来说,本月装运是绝对不可能了。情况既然如此,我们不得不请求贵方将信用证的装运期以及议付有效期分别展期至2025 年 6 月 30 日以及 7 月 15 日。

希望贵方能按我方请求尽快行动,早日给我方答复。

谨上

V. Letter writing.

Write a letter in English asking for amendments to the following letter of credit by checking it with the given contract terms.

Commercial Bank

Melbourne, Australia

Irrevocable Documentary Credit No. F-07567

Date and place of issue: August 20, 2025 Melbourne

Date and place of expiry: November 15, 2025 Melbourne

Applicant: T. G. Salgo & Co. Melbourne, Australia

Beneficiary: China National Cereals, Oils and Foodstuffs Import and Export Corporation

Advising Bank: Bank of China, Beijing

Amount: US $ 15,000.00 (Say US Dollars Fifteen Thousand Only)

Partial shipment and transshipment are prohibited.

Shipment from China Port to Melbourne, latest October 2025.

Credit available against presentation of the documents detailed herein and by your draft at sight for full invoice value.

——Signed commercial invoice in quadruplicate.

——Full set of clean on board ocean Bills of Lading made to order of Commercial Bank marked "freight prepaid".

——Insurance certificate or policy endorsed in blank for full invoice plus 10%, covering All Risks and War Risk. Covering 50,000 tins of 500 grams of Ma Ling Brand Canned Lichee at USD 3.00 per tin CFRC 2% Melbourne.

As per Contract No. SP 5432

合同主要条款:

卖方:中国粮油食品进出口公司

买方:T. G. Salgo & Co. Melbourne, Australia

商品名称:"马铃"牌荔枝罐头

规格:450 克听装

数量:50 000 听

单价:CFR 墨尔本每听 3 美元,含佣金 2%

总值:150 000.00 美元

装运期:2025 年 10 月自中国港口至墨尔本,在香港转船

付款条件:凭不可撤销即期信用证付款

合同号码:SP5432

Further Reading

扩展阅读

Letter 7: Importer Opened an L/C

Dear Sirs,

This is to inform you that we have established in line with Sales Contract No. 220 an irrevocable documentary L/C in your favor for the amount of US $ 453,000. It is valid until August 2nd, 2025.

You are authorized to draw at sight on our bank, Bank of Tokyo, against this credit for the amount of your invoice. Your draft must be accompanied by a complete set of shipping documents, consisting of:

Signed commercial invoice in three fold;

Signed packing list in three fold;

The insurance certificate in two fold for 100% invoice value plus 10%;

A full set of clean on board ocean Bills of Lading made out to order, blank endorsed.

Please check with your bank for the above L/C and notify us upon receiving the L/C.

Yours sincerely,

Letter 8: Amendment Advice

Dear Sirs,

We have received your letter asking for amendment to the L/C No. 3320. We are sorry to learn that the L/C contains several discrepancies. Anyhow, after careful study of your letter, we are now informing you that we have instructed our banker to amend the L/C accordingly. We think you will receive the L/C Amendment in due time. We trust that everything is now in order and you will be able to ship the goods in time.

Yours faithfully,

Letter 9: Reply to a Request for Payment on D/A Basis

Dear Sirs,

We received your letter of April 5, 2025 and appreciate your intention to promote the sales of our air conditioner in your country.

However, we regret that we are unable to consider your request for payment on D/A terms. As a rule, we asked for payment by L/C.

But, in view of our friendly relations, we will, as an exceptional case, accept payment for your trial order on D/P basis. In other words, we will draw on you the documentary draft at sight, through our bank, on collection basis, without L/C.

We hope the above payment terms will be acceptable to you and expect to receive your trial order in due course.

We look forward to your early reply.

Yours faithfully,

Letter 10: Buyer Insists on Payment on Collection

Dear Sirs,

Many thanks for your firm offer for 100 Princess leather handbags. The attractive designs and the superior quality will surely find a promising market in our local area.

We noticed your requirement for payment by irrevocable letter of credit, which is also our usual practice. As the leather handbags we are going to purchase are only for the coming trade show which is to be held at the beginning of next month, it is easy to see that the purchased value is well below the usual contracted figure. For such a small volume of business, it is impractical to have a letter of credit opened because the resulting charges therefore would leave a big gap to balance the profit margin. What is more, the time schedule does not allow us to have the work done at your request. Therefore, we feel necessary to insist that you draw on us at 30 days' sight on clean collection. For business larger than this in future we will be prepared to accept payment by letter of credit.

We hope you will understand our position. If the sales for promotion at our coming trade show prove profitable, hopefully you can rely on our growing import lists of more Princess handbags.

Please advise if our proposal is agreeable to you prior to 15 June.

Yours faithfully,

Letter 11: Alternative Payment Terms

Dear Sirs,

Our past purchase of steel sheets from you has been paid as a rule by confirmed, irrevocable letter of credit.

On this basis, it has indeed cost us a great deal. From the moment to open credit till the time our buyers pay us, the tie-up of our funds lasts about four months. Under the present circumstances, this question is particularly taxing owing to the tight money condition and unprecedentedly high bank interest.

If you would kindly make easier payment terms, we are sure that such an accommodation would be conductive to encouraging business. We propose either "Cash against Documents on arrival of goods" or "Drawing on us at three months' sight".

Your kindness in giving priority to the consideration of the above request and giving us an early favorable reply will be highly appreciated.

Yours faithfully,

Letter 12: Ask for Easier Terms of Payment

Dear Sirs,

We have studied the specifications and price-list of your new paints and now wish to place the enclosed order with you. As we are in urgent need of several of the items, we should be glad if you make up and ship the order as soon as you possibly can.

In the past, we have dealt with you on sight credit basis. Now, we would like to propose a different way of payment, i. e., when the goods purchased by us are ready for shipment and the freight space booked, you cable us and we will remit you the full amount by T/T. Then we can more confidently assure our buyers of the time of delivery and save a lot of expenses on opening the letter of credit. As we feel this would not make much difference to you but would facilitate our sales, we hope you will grant our request.

We look forward to your confirmation of our order and your affirmative reply to our new arrangements of payment.

Yours faithfully,

Letter 13: Inquiry for Overdue Payment

Dear Sirs,

Our two reminders about your due balance have gone unanswered.

Since you have always paid promptly, we assume that some unusual circumstance has prevented a reply.

We would appreciate your remittance by the end of this month so that we could record it and forward it to our Accounting Department with an explanation. If you have any questions, please call our sales manager directly.

Sincerely yours,

Tips

Letter of Guarantee

A letter of guarantee (L/G) is a subordinate document issued by a bank by which the issuing bank promises to the beneficiary that it will hold itself responsible for the debt, losses caused by the fault or infringement of contract of a third person. It can be used under various occasions. Here we focus on two groups: tender guarantee and performance guarantee.

Tender guarantee is issued by a bank upon the applicant of the bidder. By which the bank promises to the beneficiary (the tender inviter) it will answer for the losses caused by the bidder if he withdraws the bid or makes amendment to his bidding documents before the bidding begins, or refuses to sign or pay the margin after he has been awarded the bidding.

By a performance guarantee, the issuing bank promises to the beneficiary it will pay him a certain sum of money or adopt certain remedial measures if the principal has not duly fulfilled his liabilities in time. In international trade practices, the performance guarantee can be either supplied by the importer or the exporter. Under the former case, the issuing bank will promise to the seller that if the importer cannot duly effect payment of the goods, the bank will answer for it. As for the latter case, the issuing bank will promise to the buyer that if the exporter cannot make the delivery of the goods in time, the bank will answer for the losses sustained by the buyer.

A letter of guarantee is different from an L/C. Under the L/C, the opening bank holds itself for the payment of the goods, but under a letter of guarantee, the issuing bank holds itself responsible only after the principal has not fulfilled its obligations. Under an L/C, the seller can get the payment through negotiation, but he cannot do so under a letter of guarantee. Also, under an L/C, the issuing bank handles only the relevant documents, it has nothing to do with the sales contract, but under an L/G, when the beneficiary has presented a written documents declaring that the principal has not fulfilled his obligations and asks the issuing bank for recompense, the bank will have to make clear how and why his principal has not fulfilled his obligations. In this way, he may get involved into the disputes. As some countries, like USA and Japan, do not allow their banks to get involved in commercial disputes, the banks of these countries do not issue the L/G, instead they use standby L/C.

Chapter 9 Packing and Shipping Mark
包装与唛头

Learning Objectives

- Get a good understanding of types of packing
- Get a good understanding of shipping mark
- Grasp the techniques in writing letters concerning packing and shipping mark

学习目标:了解包装的不同类型;理解唛头的含义与构成;掌握有关包装与唛头信件的写作技巧。

Case Study

It was stipulated in the contract signed between FG and Jin Yuan that mulberry silk textile should be packed in export standard cartons of 50 pcs each. After FG established the L/C, they thought they had better remind Jin Yuan of the terms of packing. What should be mentioned in the letter?

Introduction

The recent of development of international logistics evidences the significance of packaging, especially for the packaging of goods for international transportation.

Normally, it is the exporter's responsibility to provide proper packaging for the exports, irrespective of the trade terms adopted. Proper packaging can protect the goods from the hazards of international transportation. In addition, proper packaging facilitates the handling of goods while they are in transit.

There are many modes of packaging such as case, bottle, bag, etc. To choose an appropriate mode of packaging, the exporter should consider such variables as the mode of transportation, quantity of goods, value of goods, nature of cargo, ease of handling and stowage, national requirements on weight or dimension.

Shipping marks are marks of simple designs, some letters, numbers and simple words on packages, often stenciled, which serve as an identification of the consignment to which they belong. It is one of the most important elements which are agreed on by the exporter and the importer in a sales contract.

Letters regarding packaging and shipping marks are usually required when the importer sends packaging instruction, specifies packaging requirement, asks for better packaging or enquires for packing service.

Specimen Letters
样信

Letter 1: Packing Requirement from FG

Dear Mr. Li,

We are now glad to inform you that we have opened an irrevocable letter of credit through BNP Paribas for US $ 50,000.00 in your favor.

Please make sure that mulberry silk textile should be **packed** in export standard cartons of 50 pcs each. In order to eliminate possible future trouble, we would like to stress that the packing should be in accordance with the contract.

We look forward to receiving your shipping advice.

Yours faithfully,

Letter 2: Packing Requirements

Dear Sirs,

Thank you for your letter dated April 30th about the details of packing for the goods we ordered.

In order to avoid any possible misunderstanding, we would like to inform you of the packing as follows:

All the shirts should be packed in plastic bags individually and then packed in cardboard boxes, 24 boxes to a carton, white, blue, grey, equally assorted, S/6, M/12 and L/6, 10 cartons to a wooden case. The outer packing should be strong enough to protect the goods against moisture. As the inner packing is very important to our critical customers, the cardboard boxes should be designed in a beautiful and attractive manner.

As to the outer packing, besides what you have stated, **indicative marks** like KEEP DRY, USE NO HOOKS, etc. should also be **stenciled.**

We hope you can pay special attention to the packing and our requirements on packing will not bring you much trouble.

Yours faithfully,

Letter 3: Reply (Packing Requirements)

Dear Sirs,

Thank you for your letter dated May 10 concerning packing requirements.

As requested, all the shirts will be packed in plastic bags individually and then in cardboard boxes, 24 boxes to a carton, white, blue, grey, equally assorted, S/6, M/12 and L/6, 10 cartons to a wooden case. You may rest assured that the cardboard boxes will be designed in a beautiful and attractive manner. All the cartons are to **be lined with** damp-proof paper to avoid dampness, bundled with double adhesive tapes outside.

On the wooden cases, in addition to the gross and net weights, we will mark your initials COS in a **circle**, under which the port of destination NEW YORK and contract number HP-E-01 will also be stenciled. Indicative marks like KEEP DRY, USE NO HOOKS, etc. will also be brushed.

We will arrange shipment before the end of this month and trust you will find the packing satisfactory and the goods are **in good condition** after receiving the **consignment.**

Yours faithfully,

Letter 4: Negotiation on Packing and Marking

Dear Sirs,

In reply to your letter of August 30 enquiring about the packing of our Trip Scissors, we wish to state as follows:

(1) Our export Trip Scissors are packed in boxes of one dozen each, 100 boxes to a carton.

(2) The dimensions are 17cm high, 30cm wide and 50cm long with a volume of about 0.026 cubic meters.

(3) The gross weight is 23.5kg, and the net weight is 22.5kg.

(4) In addition to the gross, net and **tare weights**, the shipping marks outside the carton should include the words "MADE IN THE PEOPLE'S REPUBLIC OF CHINA".

Should you have any special preference in this respect, please let us know and we will try our best to meet with you.

Yours faithfully,

Letter 5: Packing Instruction

Dear Sirs,

Re: Our Order No. 168

With reference to the shipment of our Order No. 168 for 100 cases of chinaware, we wish to draw your attention to the following.

As the goods are susceptible to be broken, they must be packed in wooden cases capable of withstanding rough handling.

Please mark the cases with our initials in a diamond, under which comes the destination with contract number and stencil conspicuously the words FRAGILE, HANDLE WITH CARE on both sides of the cases.

We trust that the above instructions are clear to you and that the shipment will give the users entire satisfaction.

Yours truly,

Words & Phrases 词汇

1. pack v. 包装,把……打包或装箱等

The goods are to be packed in iron drums.

货物将包装于铁桶中。

The shirts will be packed each in a polythene bag, five dozen to a cardboard case.

每件衬衫将包裹于塑料袋中,每5打装于一个纸板箱中。

常用的"包装方式"表示方式有:

(1) in...,表示用某种容器包装

Walnuts are packed in double sacks.

核桃包装于双层麻袋中。

(2) in...of...each,表示用某种容器包装,每一容器内装若干

Men's shirts are packed in wooden cases of 10 dozen each.

男士衬衫每10打装于一个木箱中。

(3) in..., each containing...,表示用某种容器包装,每一容器内装若干

Nylon's socks are packed in wooden cases, each containing 50 dozen.

尼龙袜木箱包装,每箱50打。

(4) to...,表示将若干件装于某一容器内

Folding chairs are packed 2 pieces to a carton.

两把折叠椅装一纸箱。

(5) Each...in...and...to...,表示先将每单位装入某种容器,再将若干单位装另一种较大的容器

Each pair of nylon socks is packed in a plastic bag and 12 pairs to a box.

每双尼龙袜包装于一个塑料袋中,每12双装一盒。

(6) to...and...to...,表示先将若干单位装某种容器,再把若干此种容器装另一种较大的容器

Pens are packed 12 pieces to a box and 200 boxes to a wooden case.

每12支钢笔装一个盒,每200盒装于一个木箱中。

packing n. 包装,打包,包装方法,包装材料,包装费

The packing must be seaworthy.

包装必须适合海运。

We need a lot of packing to protect these glasses.

我们需要大量的包装以保护这些眼镜。

We offer these shirts at US $20 each, plus postage and packing.

我们为衬衫报盘,每件 20 美金,包括邮寄费和包装费在内。

export packing 出口包装, improper/faulty/poor/insufficient packing 包装不良, inner packing 内包装, outer packing 外包装, packing charges/expenses 包装费, packing list 装箱单、花色码单,seaworthy packing 适合海运的包装

package n. 中小型的包裹(包、捆、束等),“一揽子”交易

Each package should be marked “Fragile”.

每件包装件上应标注“易碎品”。

The computer is sold with a printer and software as part of the package.

打印机和软件作为包装的一部分和计算机一起出售。

常见包装物:

fiber board case 纤维板箱,veneer case 胶合板箱,polyethylene bag 聚乙烯袋, jute bag 麻袋,wooden case 木箱,wooden box 木箱,crate 板条箱,skeleton case 漏孔箱,bales 捆包,sack 布袋,bag 袋, gunny bag 麻袋, paper bag 纸袋,barrel 鼓形桶, drum 铁桶,can 罐, tin 听,cylinder 钢桶,bomb 钢桶,bottle 瓶

2. mark

n. 符号,标志

shipping mark 运输标志,warning mark 警告性标志,indicative marks 指示性标志,keep cool 冷藏,keep dry 保持干燥,glass with care 小心玻璃,open here 此端打开,keep away from heat 远离热源,guard against damp 怕潮,no smoking 禁止吸烟,use no hook 请勿用钩,corrosive 腐蚀物,explosive 爆炸物,poison 有毒物, inflammable 易燃物,fragile 易碎品,perishable goods 易腐物

Please telegraph marks and destination.

请电报标志和目的地。

v. 加标志,标志

Please mark the case as per the drawing given.

请按所给图样在箱子上刷唛头。

This transaction, though small in amount, marks the beginning of our formal business relationship.

这笔交易,尽管金额不大,但标志着我们之间业务关系的开端。

3. stencil v. 用模板刷制(唛头)

We will stencil the shipping marks in accordance with your instructions.

我们将按照贵方的要求刷唛头。

Please note the warning marks like "Poison" and "Inflammable", etc. should be stenciled on the outer packing.

请注意诸如"有毒物""易燃物"这样的警告性标志应刷在外包装上。

4. circle n. 圆形

常用于唛头中的图形有:square 正方形,triangle 三角形,rectangle 长方形,oval 椭圆形,heart 心形,downward triangle 倒三角形,pear-shaped 葫芦形,parallelogram 平行四边形,trapezoid 梯形

5. line

v. 衬里,安排

lined with thin paper 内衬薄纸

lined with kraft paper 内衬牛皮纸

lined with moist proof paper & kraft paper 内衬防潮纸、牛皮纸

Please line the cases with wax paper.

请将箱子内衬蜡纸。

We may be able to line up 50 metric tons for you in the next few days.

我们几天后能给贵方安排 50 公吨。

n. 短函,行业,(一类)货色

As soon as you reach a decision, please drop us a line.

一旦贵方做出决定,请给我们发一短函。

We have been for many years in the chemical line.

我们在化工品领域很多年。

This is a good line of hardware.

这是五金中的一类好货。

in line (out of line)相符合(不相符合)

Your price is quite in line, but the time of shipment is too extended.

贵方的价格合理,但装运期太长了。

Your price is entirely out of line with the market.

贵方的价格完全与市场不符。

6. in good condition 状况良好

类似的表述有:in perfect/sound condition 状态良好,in a damaged condition 损坏状态,in a mouldy condition 受潮状态

The goods arrived in good condition.

货物到达时状况良好。

7. consignment n.

(1)托运,发运,运送

We will ship all the twenty sets in one consignment.

我们将一次装运 20 台。

(2)寄售,寄售的货物

We cannot ship the goods on consignment.

我们不能以寄售方式装运货物。

(3)托运的货物,一批交付的货物,货物

It is expected that the consignment will be ready for shipment early next month.

预计货物将在下月初备妥待运。

8. tare weight n. 皮重

类似的表述有:net weight 净重,gross weight 毛重

Useful Sentences 常用句型

1. The full details regarding packing and marking must be strictly observed.

请严格遵守包装及运输标志的详细内容。

2. Packing of our men's shirts is each in a poly bag, 5 dozen to a carton lined with waterproof paper and bound with two iron straps outside.

我们男式衬衫的包装为每一件装于一个塑料袋,每 5 打装一个带有防水纸内衬的纸箱,外边由两条铁皮带加固。

3. We are afraid that we shall have to charge more for the designated packing,

as it calls for extra labor and cost.

对指定的包装我们恐怕要收取更多的费用，因为这需要花费额外的劳动力和成本。

4. After a check-up by our staff at the warehouse it was found that some bags had not been repacked in 5-ply strong paper bags as stipulated in the contract, thus resulting in the breakage during transit.

我们的员工在仓库检查后发现一些袋子尚未按合同规定改装为 5 层厚的牢固纸袋，从而导致运输过程中的破损。

5. As the boxes are possible to receive rough handling at this end, you must see to it that packing is strong enough to protect the goods.

由于箱子在此地可能会遭到野蛮的装卸，贵方必须确保包装足够坚固以保护货物。

6. We suggest that the goods should be repacked in neutral packing. Please inform us whether it can be accepted or not.

我们提议货物应再包装为中性包装。请告知贵方能否接受。

7. The packing of the goods must be improved in order to fit for seaworthy condition.

货物的包装必须改进以适合海运。

8. In order to eliminate possible future trouble, we would like to make clear beforehand our packing requirements as follows.

为了避免以后可能的麻烦，我们想预先明确我们如下的包装要求。

9. We shall appreciate it if you will inform us of the condition of packing as soon as the consignment arrives at your end.

如果货物一到达贵方，贵方就能告知我们包装的状况，我们将不胜感激。

10. Please mark our initials SCC in a diamond, under which the port of destination and our order number should be stenciled. In addition, warning marks like KEEP DRY, USE NO HOOK, etc. should also be indicated.

请将我们的首字母 SCC 刷在一个菱形标志内，紧接其后为目的港和订单号。另外，诸如"保持干燥""请勿用钩"等警告标志也应刷上。

11. Our packing is standardized in a manner which has proved successful in

export shipment.

我们的包装方式在出口装运上已经成功证实为标准方式。

12. The new packing for our porcelain is in Chinese national style and suitable for display in supermarket.

我们瓷器的新包装具有中国特色,并适合在超市陈列。

13. Cartons are comparatively light and compact, more convenient to handle in the course of loading and unloading, quite fit for ocean transportation. As a kind of packing container, they have been extensively used in international trade.

纸箱比较轻,结构紧凑,更方便装卸,很适合海洋运输。作为一种包装容器,它们已经在国际贸易中被广泛利用。

14. We are sorry that we are unable to comply with your request for special packing, but would like to make the following suggestion for your consideration.

很抱歉,我们不能满足贵方所提出的特别包装要求,但愿意提出如下建议供贵方参考。

15. The new packaging of this article is designed in a special manner and we are confident that it will appeal strongly to consumers.

该商品的新包装是以特殊方式设计的,我们相信它将能对消费者产生强烈的吸引力。

Exercises 练习

Ⅰ. Translate the following sentences into Chinese.

1. The wooden case should be not only seaworthy but also strong enough to protect the goods from damage.

2. Every 100 dozen should be packed in a wooden case marked TM and numbered from No. 1 upward.

3. On the outer packing, please mark "HANDLE WITH CARE" and "KEEP COOL".

4. We must make it clear that with the different packing materials the packing expenses will be different.

5. For better results, we now use plastic bags instead of paper ones, which not

only gives better protection but also adds to the attraction of the goods.

6. The continuing increases in freight costs force us to seek improved packing methods. Could you suggest a more economical packing method for our products?

7. Our clients would like to have the products packed in window packing for inner packing so that the products can be seen directly.

8. We are of the opinion that if the result of packing in cartons turns out to the satisfaction of our clients, you may continue using this packing in future. However, in case of the result not being so, we are afraid that this will considerately affect the development of business between us.

9. As far as the marking is concerned, please mark the bales with our initials as well as the port of destination and the contract number as follows.

10. We will take every step within our reach to improve the packing so as to protect the goods from breakage.

Ⅱ. Translate the following sentences into English.

1. 跟以前一样,箱子上要刷制一个菱形标志,内写我公司的首字母。

2. 我们想把纸板箱包装改为木箱包装。

3. 请对包装特别注意,否则,货物将会在运输途中损坏。

4. 贵方产品质量很好,但内包装质量太差,不能引起顾客的注意。对我们今后的订货,请改进包装。

5. 货物要转运,所以我们希望每个箱体上标注重量说明、警告性标志、指示性标志及贵方自己的标志。

6. 附上我方货物包装所用的唛头,并请在刷唛头时做到清楚、正确。

7. 所有布袋都有防水内衬,以保护货物。

8. 请采用必要保护,以使货物不致受潮及雨淋,因为这些衬衫易于在运输途中受潮或雨淋而损坏。

9. 包装和唛头由卖方决定,包装费用一般由买方负担。

10. 这批货物我方建议改用中性包装,请告知可否接受。

Ⅲ. Translate the following letter into Chinese.

Dear Sirs,

On May 20th, we received your consignment of 40 cardboard cartons of steel screws.

We regret to inform you that 10 cartons were delivered damaged and the contents had spilled.

We accept that the damage was not your fault but feel it necessary that you must modify our packing to avoid future losses.

We require that future packing be in wooden cases of 20 kilos net, each wooden case containing 40 cardboard boxes of 500 grams net.

Please let us know whether these specifications can be met by you and whether they will lead to an increase in your prices.

We look forward to your early confirmation.

Yours faithfully,

Ⅳ. Translate the following letter into English.

敬启者：

事由：第 99 号售货确认书

感谢贵方 10 月 10 日的来信以及随函附寄的一式两份的标题项下的售货确认书，但发现合同中的包装条款不够清晰。相关的条款应为：

包装：适合长途运输的海运包装

标题合同项下的衬衫应包装于塑料袋中，每五打装一箱，每二十箱装一托盘，每十托盘装一集装箱。在外包装上，请将我们名称的首字母缩写标注于一个三角形中，紧随其下是目的港和我们的订单号。此外，诸如“防水”这样的指示性标示也请注明。

我们希望贵方能对包装给予特别的关注，期待不久收到贵方的装船通知。

谨上

Ⅴ. Letter writing.

Write a letter of negotiation on packing and marking.

Further Reading

扩展阅读

Letter 6: Comments on Packing the Goods in Cartons

Dear Sirs,

It gives us much pleasure to advise you that 500 dozen Shirts under Order No. SC-86 packed in cartons were shipped on board SS Peace on 25th July to be transshipped at Hong Kong. We shall appreciate it if you will inform us of the condition of packing as soon as the consignment arrives at your end.

In regard to the packing of the goods in question in cartons, we wish to give you our comments as follows:

1. Packing in cartons prevents skilful pilferage. As the trace of pilferage will be more in evidence, the insurance company may be made to pay the necessary compensation for such losses.

2. Cartons are quite fit for ocean transportation, and they are extensively used in our shipments to other ports to the entire satisfaction of our clients. Such packing has also been accepted by our insurance company against WPA and TPND.

3. These cartons are well protected against moisture by plastic lining. The very fact that they are made of paperboard induces special attention in handling and storage. Thus shirts packed in such cartons are not as susceptible to damage by moisture as those packed in wooden cases.

4. Since cartons are comparatively light and compact, they are more convenient for handling in loading and unloading. Besides, they are not likely to be mixed with wooden cases in transport or storage, so that the rate of breakage is lower than that of wooden cases.

In view of the above reasons, it is believed that your clients will find packing in cartons satisfactory and their fears unwarranted.

We are awaiting your further comments.

Yours truly,

Letter 7: Asking for Improving Packing

Dear Sirs,

Thank you for your quotation No. 20 about round steel bars.

We regret to inform you that among the five lots of round steel bars arriving here per S. S. Peace on May 2nd, 2025 there were six bundles of different grades, which were in scattered and mixed condition because their packing was not sufficiently strong and their iron hoops were broken in transit. Since it was very difficult to assort them, inconvenience and losses occurred. Although we had in time notified you of such unfortunate things before, the present case has shown that our comments were ignored, for no improvements in packing have been made.

Therefore, we must have your promise to take effective measures to improve your packing before we could book the new order with you.

We await your early reply.

Yours sincerely,

Tips

Packing

When an order is received from abroad, the exporter gets the goods ready for shipment. It is most important for him to see that the goods are suitably packed. Associated with packing is the marking of the goods. The outer packing must be marked clearly with the identifying symbols and numbers in accordance with the instructions of the importer in order to enable the customs authorities, the steamship clerks and the importer to identify the packages en route or at the port of destination. In marking and numbering packages it is essential that the mark (or symbol) and numbers conform in every respect to those written in the commercial invoice, the consular invoice, the bill of lading and the other shipping documents used. The best method of marking is to stencil the marks on the outside of the package. Generally, marks are classified into three categories: shipping mark, supplementary (or additional) mark, and indicative (or warning) mark.

In most cases, shipping mark consists of the name of the consignee or shipper, destination and packing number. Symbols with a simple identity code or initials are often used instead of writing out the full name of the consignee in order not to disclose the consignee's name. Below the name of the destination is usually placed the package number. Packages may be numbered consecutively or marked merely with a total number.

Sometimes according to the stipulations of the relative regulations or laws of the importing country, or upon request of the importer, it is the practice to supply the supplementary mark giving the dimensions of the package which may be used in Customs entry or in assessing the freight. It is preferable for the gross and net weights to be shown.

To facilitate handling or to warn the crew against dangerous cargoes or to overcome different language problems recognized marking terms are used, such as "HANDLE WITH CARE" "FRAGILE" "USE NO HOOKS" "KEEP COOL" which are known as indicative mark. Sometimes the following known as warning marks may be printed on the outer package, such as "POISON" "EXPLOSIVE" "HAZARDOUS ARTICLE".

Chapter 10 Shipment
装运

Learning Objectives

- Know what shipping documents are.
- Get a good understanding of the definition, contents, functions and types of B/L.
- Grasp the techniques in writing letters concerning shipment.

学习目标:了解装运单据的含义;理解提单的定义、内容、作用和类型;掌握有关装运信件的写作技巧。

Case Study

On April 12, 2025, the manager of the transport department asked the staff to contact the forwarding agent to arrange for shipment based on the Contract No. FG20250112 and the L/C No. LC000123756. After the goods were shipped on board, Jin Yuan sent the shipping advice to FG. What should be included in such a letter?

Introduction

Shipment or transportation of traded goods nowadays is a very important part in foreign trade.

There are many means of transportation and each has its advantages and disadvantages. Goods can be transported by train, truck, plane, ship or through pipeline, depending on the nature of the goods, the time requirement, the cost, etc. However, ships are still the most important means of transportation in international trade. About 90% of world trade is conveyed by sea transportation. Container transportation has grown to be a code of more convenient way of conveying goods.

Shipment clauses usually include shipment time, port of shipment, port of destination, shipping documents, partial shipment and transshipment.

A number of documents are required for shipping. The primary documents are bill of lading, commercial invoice, insurance policy, inspection certificate, packing list, etc. Among these, the most important shipping document is the bill of lading.

A bill of lading is a type of document that is used to acknowledge the receipt of shipment of goods and is a certificate of ownership of goods. The B/L thus serves three important purposes, namely: 1) the receipt of goods carried; 2) the evidence of contract to carry goods; 3) a documentary proof of ownership of the goods. If the cargo is apparently in good order and properly packed when received by the shipping company, the bill of lading is deemed as "clean". Normally, a clean B/L is required by the importers and will be vital for the exporters to get the payment.

Major types of correspondence in shipping include the letters on the buyer's shipping instruction, the letters on the seller's shipping advice, the letters urging prompt delivery, the letters amending shipping terms or the letters apologizing for late shipment.

Specimen Letters

样信

Letter 1: Shipping Advice from Jin Yuan

Dear Mr. Brown,

Re: Contract No. FG20250112 Covering 20,000 pcs Mulberry Silk Textile

We have pleasure in informing you that we have **shipped the above goods on board per S. S.** Peace this morning in accordance with the stipulations in the captioned contract. The goods are expected to reach Marseille on or about April 24.

Enclosed please find a copy of **the shipping documents.** We trust this **consignment** will reach you in sound condition and look forward to cooperating with you again soon.

Yours faithfully,

Encl.

Letter 2: Shipping Instruction

Dear Sirs,

As having informed you by fax on 6th March, we have booked **shipping space** on S. S. Peace for the first lot under our contract No. 345. This vessel is **scheduled** to leave for Singapore by the end of this month.

For future instructions, you should get in touch with our shipping agents in Singapore.

We consider it our duty to remind you of the time limit of shipment as stipulated in our contract, say 31st March. We hope that the goods will be duly shipped on board. If not, **dead freight** or **demurrage** should be for your account.

Yours truly,

Letter 3: Shipping Advice

Dear Sirs,

Re: Our L/C No. 345

We are pleased to advise you that we have shipped the goods on board in accordance with the stipulations set forth in captioned Letter of Credit by **MV Peace**. We are informed by the shipping company that the ship is scheduled to arrive at your port on or about April 5th.

We are sending you **under cover** one duplicate set of **shipping documents**, so you may make all the necessary preparations to **take delivery** of the goods when they duly arrive at your port, which include: invoice, packing list, inspection certificate of quality, insurance policy and bill of lading.

We trust **the above shipment** will reach you in sound condition and expect to receive your further orders soon.

We appreciate the business you have been able to secure for us and assure you that all your future correspondence enquiries and orders will continue to receive our prompt attention.

Yours truly,

Encl.

Letter 4: Urging Prompt Delivery

Dear Sirs,

With reference to our correspondences, we would like to remind you that the goods should have been delivered by the end of May. However, up to now we have not received the shipment, nor have we received shipping advice about the goods.

As our end-users are in urgent need of the goods, we request that the goods should be delivered by the first half of June. If you cannot deliver the goods by this time, we would **reserve the right to cancel the contract** and you will be responsible for all the losses arising as a result of your failure to do so.

Please let us have your favorable reply without any delay.

Yours faithfully,

Letter 5: Apologizing for Late Shipment

Dear Sirs,

We have received your letter dated June 3, in which you asked for our favorable reply about the shipment of your order No. 334.

Upon receipt of your letter, we contacted our shipping agent. Unfortunately, we are told that there is no enough shipping space for your order by the first half of June. If possible, we can deliver 2,000 pieces on or before 13 June and **the remainder** by end June.

Enclosed please find our amendment advice for extension of delivery and that of L/C. We regret for any inconvenience to you for the delay of shipment.

Yours faithfully,

Encl.

Letter 6: E-mail for Shipping details for Numan MP4, M6000

To:

Cc:

From:

Subject: Re: Shipping details for Numan MP4, M6000

Dear John,

Regarding our Numan MP4, M6000, I'm so affirmative that their quality was substantially upgraded.

As for shipment, I have contacted our shipping forwarder and was informed the **cargo cut-off date** would be next Wednesday.

The **CBM** for this order is just 18.2, not enough for a full 20' container. Would you like to adopt shipment by **LCL** or **FCL**?

Awaiting your early reply.

Best regards,

Words & Phrases 词汇

1. shipped the goods on board 货物已装船

2. per prep. 由……装运来(出口商角度)

We have shipped 100 metric tons of wool per S. S. Rose.

我们已通过“玫瑰”轮装运100公吨的羊毛。

ex prep. 从……,在……装运(进口商角度)

The goods ex S. S. Wuxi have been re-inspected.

由“无锡”轮运来的货物已经复检。

by prep. 由某轮承运

Your order No. 3421 will be shipped by S. S. Manchester.

贵方第3421号订单下的货物将由“曼彻斯特”轮承运。

3. S. S steamship 轮船

4. consignment n. 运送,运送的货物,托运,寄售

consign v. 托运,交付

The consignment should reach you by end May.

货物将在 5 月底到达贵方。

5. shipping n. 运输

shipping instruction 装船须知,shipping space 舱位,shipping advice 装船通知,shipping documents 运输单据,shipping line 船公司,shipping agent 船务代理人

We are sending you herewith a full set of shipping documents.

我们寄给贵方一整套的装运单据。

shipment n. 装船,装运

prompt shipment 立即发货,partial shipment 分批装运,date of shipment 发货日期,port of shipment 发货港,装运港

6. schedule v. 按计划 n. 时间表,计划表,日程安排

be scheduled to = due to 预计

This vessel is scheduled to leave for London on Tuesday.

这条船预计星期二驶往伦敦。

This vessel is due to arrive at Shanghai Port at the beginning of next month.

这条船预期于下月初抵达上海港。

7. dead freight 空舱费

8. demurrage n. 滞期费

despatch money 速遣费

It is understood that all Charter Parties involved under this Contract shall stipulate that dispatch money to be half the demurrage for all working days saved at loading port.

本合同项下的所有租船契约内均应列明,因在装运港节省装运时间而支付的速遣费应为滞期费的一半。

9. mv motor vessel 轮船

10. under cover 随函

under separate cover 另邮,另寄

We are sending you under cover a copy of catalogue.

我们随函附寄给贵方一份商品目录。

We are sending you our catalogue under separate cover.

我们将另邮给贵方一份商品目录。

11. shipping documents 装运单据

12. take delivery 提货 take delivery of the goods

When can we take delivery of our order?

我们什么时候可以提货?

13. above shipment 上述货物

shipment n. 装运的货物,装运

We have inspected the shipment ex S. S. Peace.

我们检验了由"和平"号装运的货物。

The goods are all ready for shipment.

货物备妥待运。

14. reserve the right to cancel the contract 保留取消合同的权利

15. remainder n. 剩余的商品 remains, remaining

The remaining is going to be shipped by the first available steamer next month.

剩下的货物下月将通过首条可利用的船只装运。

16. cargo cut-off date 货物截关日

17. CBM, cubic meter 的简写,立方米

18. LCL, less than container load 拼箱货

FCL, full container load 整箱货

Useful Sentences 常用句型

1. We are glad to inform you that the goods ordered by you are ready for delivery. Shipment can be made immediately after receipt of L/C.

我们很高兴地告知贵方,贵方所订购的货物已经备妥待运。我们收到信用证后可以立即安排装运。

2. We shall cable you in due course the name of the chartered steamer and its expected date of arrival at your port to enable you to take delivery of the goods in

time.

我们将在适当的时间致电告知贵方所租船名、预计到达贵方港口的时间，以便贵方及时提货。

3. As the shipment date stipulated in the L/C is by July 3 and cannot be further extended, the goods must be shipped not later than the above date.

由于信用证中规定的装运日期是 7 月 3 日前并且不能延期，所以货物不得迟于上述日期装船。

4. As most of the items on this order are not yet ready for shipment, we would ask you to permit partial shipments in your L/C to enable us to ship first the part which is ready for shipment.

由于订单上大多数的商品还没有备好待运，我们想请求贵方的信用证允许分批装运以便我们先装运已备好待运的部分。

5. We herewith send you the goods ordered last week, and hope you will find same satisfactory. Your further orders will receive our prompt attention.

我们随函寄出贵方上周所订的货物，希望贵方能认为它们是令人满意的。贵方随后的订单也会受到我们及时的关注。

6. As your prompt attention to shipment is most desirable to all parties concerned, we hope you will let us have your shipping advice by fax without further delay.

由于相关各方都希望贵方能对装运密切关注，我们希望贵方能立即以传真方式发出装运通知。

7. Owing to the delay in opening the relevant L/C, shipment cannot be made as contracted and should be postponed to March 5.

由于在开立相关信用证上的延误，装运不能按合同安排，将要被推迟到 3 月 5 日。

8. Kindly accept our thanks for your extension of your L/C No. 223 and we are now pleased to inform you that we have this day shipped the above goods on board mv Peace which sails for your port tomorrow.

请接受我们对贵方将第 223 号信用证展期的谢意。我们很高兴地告知贵方，今天已将上述货物装上“和平”号，该船明天驶往贵方港口。

9. Owing to the delay of the scheduled steamer, we have failed to effect shipment within the L/C validity. Would you please extend the shipment of the L/C for one month to enable us to proceed with shipment as quickly as possible?

由于所预订轮船的延误,我们未能在信用证有效期内安排装运。请将信用证的装运展期一个月以便我们能够尽快着手装船。

10. The goods will be ready for shipment by the end of this month. Please notify us at an early date of the name of the chartered steamer and its date of arrival at our port.

货物将于本月底备运。请尽早通知我们所租船只的名称以及到达我方港口的日期。

11. Please book the necessary shipping space to ensure timely dispatch of the goods ordered.

请预订所需的舱位以确保能及时装运所订购的货物。

12. It is stipulated in the contract No. 730 that shipment is to be made in Aug. However something unexpected compels us to seek your cooperation by advancing shipment of the goods from Aug. to July. We shall appreciate your advancing shipment to July.

第 730 号合同规定 8 月份安排装运。然而一些意外的情况迫使我们寻求贵方的合作,将装运期从 8 月份提前至 7 月份。如果贵方能同意,我们将不胜感激。

13. Since there is no direct steamer sailing to your port prior to August 5, we are extremely sorry for our inability to advance the shipment as requested.

由于从此地到贵方港口 8 月 5 日前没有直达船,非常抱歉我们不能按照要求提前装运。

Exercises 练习

Ⅰ. Translate the following sentences into Chinese.

1. We wish to advise you that the goods under S/C No. 342 have been shipped on board per steamer Peace on Dec. 23, 2024 to be transshipped in Singapore and expected to reach your port early Jan. 2025.

2. The earliest shipment is in August. We hope this will be acceptable to your customers.

3. Since the purchase is made on FOB basis, you are to ship the goods from Singapore on a steamer to be designated by us.

4. As the market is sluggish, please postpone the shipment of our order goods to March.

5. If you desire earlier delivery, we can only make a partial shipment of 50 metric tons of steels in July and the balance of 50 metric tons in August.

6. If you do not deliver the goods by this time, we must cancel this contract and claim remedies accordingly.

7. As the deadline for shipment stipulated in the relevant L/C is on or before July 1, please quote us for a shipping container from Shanghai to New York before that date.

8. For your information, S. S. Mermaid is scheduled to sail from Shanghai to New York on or about 15 July. Please let us know if you wish to ship ten cases of art goods by that ship.

9. Please book the shipping container for the goods and let us know the ocean freight as soon as possible.

10. Please note that partial shipments and transshipment are not permitted.

Ⅱ. Translate the following sentences into English.

1. 上述订购货物已备齐,请早日指示如何发运。

2. 贵公司上周所订购的货物已发运,希望贵公司会感到满意。

3. 合同规定一旦货物装船,卖方须电告装运通知。

4. 在收到贵方信用证修改通知书以后,我们立即预订该船的舱位。

5. 我方要求立即交货,否则我方将不得不按合同规定取消订货。

6. 由于发生一些意外情况,我方提请贵方将第 234 号订单下货物的装运期从 10 月份提前到 9 月份。

7. 我方客户急需此货,务请贵方在合同规定的期限内交货。

8. 希望此批货物能完好无损地顺利到达目的港,以满足贵方的需要。

9. 对于此次我方无法控制的延误,我方深表遗憾。

10. 我们想提醒贵方,货物需按信用证规定在 10 月 20 日前发运,否则,对因延误交货而可能造成的任何损失,贵方必须负责。

Ⅲ. Translate the following letter into Chinese.

Dear Sirs,

We are in receipt of your letter of August 10th, in which you asked us to advance the shipment of your order for bicycles to August 20th.

On receiving your letter, we immediately contact the shipping agent. Unfortunately, we are told that there is no enough space for your order during the rest August. If you desire an earlier delivery, we can only deliver 200 cartons in August and the remainder in September.

Kindly let us know your opinion as soon as possible.

Yours faithfully,

Ⅳ. Translate the following letter into English.

敬启者:

事由:第123号购货合同

收到贵方6月25日的来信,想要获知标题项下货物装运的确切消息。

由于现在是装运的高峰期,我们自己也正在等候本地货代关于舱位的答复,因此目前不能给予任何好消息。但我们将尽力在相关信用证到期前交货。

对于舱位不足导致延误的任何不便我们深感遗憾。我们期待近期能以传真方式将我们努力的结果告知贵方。

谨上

Ⅴ. Letter writing.

Suppose your company should deliver the goods to the importer in one lot. As there is no sufficient shipping space at present, you should persuade your customer to accept partial shipments. What should be included in such letters?

Further Reading
扩展阅读

Letter 7: Giving Shipping Instructions to the Seller

Dear Sirs,

We acknowledge your Sales Contract No. 998 in duplicate for 5,000 pieces of men's shirts.

Although the price in the Contract is quoted on FOB basis, we should appreciate it if you could arrange for the contract of carriage with the carrier on usual terms at our risk and account.

When the shipping space is booked, please advise us of the name and voyage number of the vessel, B/L number, estimated time of departure, estimated time of arrival and any other information necessary for us to cover insurance at our end.

Your close cooperation about the above is highly appreciated.

Yours sincerely,

Letter 8: Loading Letter

Dear Sirs,

MV Peace arrived at Antwerp yesterday at 5 : 30 pm and will be ready to start loading at 2 : 00 pm today, 30 May, 2025.

Loading is expected to be completed on Monday. Then the vessel will go to another berth in Antwerp Dock for loading of a number of cranes which are to be discharged at Mombasa. Loading all Antwerp cargo is expected to end on 14 June. The estimated time of arrival in Xingang given by the vessel is 27 June.

We hope you will find the above helpful.

Yours faithfully,

Letter 9: Enquiry for Shipping Containers

Dear Sirs,

We have ten cases of arts and crafts at the above address ready for dispatch to London, and shall be glad if you will arrange for your shipping container to collect them. Each case weighs 40 kg.

As the L/C stipulates that shipment be not later than 8 August, please quote us for a shipping container from Xingang to London before that deadline.

Your early quotation will be appreciated.

Yours faithfully,

Letter 10: Quotation of a Container

Dear Sirs,

Thank you for your fax of 3rd July, in which you asked us to quote shipping container to London for ten cases of arts and crafts.

The shipping containers we provide are of two sizes, namely 10 ft. and 20 ft. long and built to take loads up to two to four tons respectively. They can be opened at both ends, thus it is possible to load and unload them at the same time. They are both watertight and airtight and can be loaded and locked at the factory, if necessary.

There is also a saving in freight charges when separate consignments intended for the same port of destination are carried in one container and an additional saving on insurance because of the lower premiums charged for container shipped goods.

We enclose a copy of our tariff and look forward to receiving your instructions.

Yours faithfully,

Encl.

Letter 11: Requesting Postponement of Shipment

Dear Sirs,

In regard to the first shipment against our Contract No. 123, we wrote to you on 3rd July that part of the goods were not in conformity with the contracted specifications. We requested you to advise us on how you would like to deal with the matter, but up to now we have not yet received any reply.

So we regret to declare that we can not bind ourselves to accept the second lot, which is scheduled to be delivered by the end of next month unless the quality has been improved. We have to request that you should postpone shipment of the contract for the time being. It goes without saying that we have no obligations whatever in this matter.

Meanwhile, we are still looking forward to your reply.

Yours faithfully,

Tips

Partial Shipment and Transshipment

In case of an export business covering a large amount of goods it is necessary to make shipment in several lots by several carriers sailing on different dates. This is done because of the limitation of shipping space available, poor unloading facilities at the port of destination, a dull market season, or possible delay in the process of manufacturing of the goods, etc. This is allowable only if the clause "Partial shipment to be allowed" is agreed upon in the sales contract. If partial shipment is not permitted, the clause "No partial shipment" or its like should be inserted in the contract.

Transshipment, in ocean shipping, is the movement of the goods in transit from one carrier to another at the ports of transshipment before the goods reach the port of destination. Transshipment is necessary when ships sailing direct to the port of destination are not available, the port of destination does not lie along the sailing route of the liner, or the amount of cargo for a certain port of destination is so small that no ships would like to call at that port. With a clause like "Transshipment to be allowed" stated in the contract, transshipment is permissible, then.

Generally speaking, partial shipment or transshipment is favorable to the seller, which shall put the seller in a better position to perform the relevant contract. According to the relevant stipulations of the UCP, transport documents which appear on their faces to indicate that shipment has been made on the same means of conveyance and the same journey for the same destination, will not be regarded as partial shipments, even if the transport documents indicate different dates of issuance and/or different ports of shipment, places of taking in charge, or dispatch. According to the relevant stipulations of the "Uniform Customs and Practice for Documentary Credits", if any installment is not shipped within the period allowed for that installment, the credit ceases to be available for that and any subsequent installments, unless otherwise stipulated in the contract.

Chapter 11 Insurance
保险

Learning Objectives

- Know the definition and classification of insurance
- Grasp the steps in writing letters on insurance

学习目标:了解保险的定义与分类;掌握保险信件的写作步骤。

Case Study

According to the contract signed between Jin Yuan and FG, the goods should be covered by the Sellers for 110% of full invoice value against All Risks. However, FG wrote to Jin Yuan asking for insurance for 120% of the invoice value. Could such request be accepted? What could Jin Yuan do?

Introduction

In international trade, the goods traveling long distances to another country may face all kinds of risks or losses as they are out of the direct physical control of both the buyer and the seller; therefore, they must be insured against loss or damage at each stage of their journey.

In a contract of insurance, two parties are involved: insurer and insured. Insurer refers to the party who promises to indemnify losses or provide service, namely, the insurance company or the individual who runs an insurance firm. Insured refers to the party who covers insurance from the insurer or the insurance company, namely, the buyer, the seller, or the shipping company.

The clause of insurance mainly consists of coverage, the insurance amount and premium.

There is a wide range of coverage with the following three basic ones: Free of Particular Average (FPA), With Particular Average (WPA) or With Particular (WP), All Risks. General additional risks usually consist of theft, pilferage, and non-delivery (TPND), fresh water and/or rain water damage, risks of shortage, risks of hook damage, risk of breakage, etc. Special additional risks consist of failure to delivery risks, war risks, strikes, riots and civil commotions (SRCC), etc.

When writing a letter covering effecting insurance, one should indicate the consignment, the amount of insurance, the coverage of the insurance, the premium rate, the insurance company, etc.

Specimen Letters
样信

Letter 1: Reply to Extra Coverage from FG

Dear Mr. Brown,

Re: Contract No. FG20250112 Covering 20,000 pcs Mulberry Silk Textile

We acknowledge your letter of April 18, in which you requested us to **effect insurance** for 120% of the invoice value.

We would like to make it clear that it is our usual practice to insure on the goods for 110% of the invoice value. Extra coverage, if desired, can also be arranged **on condition that** the extra **premium** concerned is for the customer's account. So the difference between 110% and 120% should be at your cost.

Upon receipt of your affirmative reply, we will cover insurance for the captioned goods without any delay.

Yours faithfully,

Letter 2: Importer Asks Exporter to Cover Insurance

Dear Sirs,

Re: Insurance on Shandong Groundnuts

Referring to our Purchase Order No. 99 for 500 M/Ts Shandong Groundnuts, you will find that this order is concluded on FOB basis.

However, we now desire to have the goods insured **at your end**. It will be highly appreciated if you will kindly have the goods covered for our account against All Risks and Aflatoxin Risk at invoice value plus 10%, i. e. US $ 500,000. Upon receipt of your debit note, of course, we will **refund the premium to you** or you may draw a draft at sight on us for the same.

Please take note of the above and we sincerely hope that our request will meet your approval.

Yours faithfully,

Letter 3: Reply to the Above Request

Dear Sirs,

Re: Insurance on Shandong Groundnuts

We have received your letter dated Sep. 23rd, in which you asked us to insure the captioned goods for an amount of 10% above the invoice value for your account.

In reply, we confirm having insured the goods with the PICC for 110% of the invoice value against All Risks and Aflatoxin Risk as per the CIC dated Jan. 1, 1981. The insurance policy is being prepared accordingly and we will forward it to you later together with **the debit note** for the premium.

For your information, we are glad to tell you that the goods have been ready for shipment and they will be loaded on board S. S. Peace due to sail to your port on or about Oct. 5.

Yours faithfully,

Letter 4: Importer's Request for Additional Insurance Amount

Dear Sirs,

Referring to our Order No. 123 covering 2,000 Electric Heaters, we are pleased to inform you that we have established the confirmed, irrevocable L/C No. 321 with the Bank of China, New York for the amount of US $ 100,000, valid until Nov. 23.

Please see to it that the above-mentioned order should be shipped around early November and the goods should be covered for 120% of the invoice value against All Risks. As we know, it is your customary practice to insure the goods for 10% above the invoice value and the extra premium for additional amount shall be for our account.

It will be appreciated if you could arrange insurance according to our request and meanwhile we are expecting your shipping advice.

Yours sincerely,

Letter 5: Reply to the Above Request

Dear Sirs,

Re: Your Order No. 123 covering 2,000 Electric Heaters

We acknowledge your letter of Sep. 12nd, in which you asked us to insure the captioned order for an amount of 20% above the invoice value.

As we usually arrange to **take out the insurance** for the invoice value plus 10%, we are prepared to comply with your request for insuring the goods for 120% of the invoice value against All Risks. But we should remind you that the extra premium will be for your account.

Yours faithfully,

Letter 6: Application for Insurance

Dear Sirs,

We shall have a consignment of electric heaters valued at US $ 100,000 CIF vessel Singapore, to be shipped from Boston by S. S. Peace sailing around 29 October.

We wish to cover the goods with your company against All Risks from our warehouse to Singapore for 120% of the invoice value. We shall appreciate it if you could quote your favorable rate for the cover.

Yours truly,

Words & Phrases 词汇

1. arrange to take out the insurance 办理保险

All Risks 一切险，是中国人民财产保险股份有限公司(PICC)制定的中国保险条款中的《海洋运输货物保险条款》所包括的三个基本险别之一，其他两个险别为平安险(Free from Particular Average, FPA)和水渍险(With Particular Average, WPA)。除这三种基本险别外，还有附加险(Extraneous Risks)，包括一般附加险、特殊附加险和特别附加险。

常见的一般附加险有 11 种，分别为：

Theft, Pilferage and Non-delivery Risks (TPND)偷窃、提货不着险

Fresh and/or Rain Water Damage Risks 淡水雨淋险

Shortage Risk/Risk of Shortage 短量险

Intermixture and Contamination Risks 混杂、沾污险

Leakage Risk/Risk of Leakage 渗漏险

Clash and Breakage Risks 碰损、破碎险

Hook Damage Risk 钩损险

Rust Risk/Risk of Rust 锈损险

Breakage of Packing Risk 包装破裂险

Sweating and Heating Risks 受潮受热险

Taint of Odor Risks 串味险

常见的特殊附加险有两种，分别为：

War Risk 战争险

Strikes, Riots, Civil Commotion (SRCC)罢工险

常见的特别附加险有 6 种，包括：

Import Duty Risk 进口关税险

Failure to Delivery Risk 交货不到险

On Deck Risk 舱面险

Rejection Risk 拒收险

Aflatoxin Risk 黄曲霉素险

FREC 出口货物到香港(包括九龙在内)或澳门存仓火险责任扩展条款

2. insure v. 投保，办理保险

Please insure against Shortage Risk.

请投保短量险。

Please insure the goods against All Risks and War Risk.

请为货物投保一切险和战争险。

insurance n. 保险，常与 insurance 搭配的动词或动词词组有：to arrange/cover/effect/provide/take out insurance 办理保险，投保

表示投保的货物，用 insurance on+所投保的货物，如 insurance on the 500 sets of Electric Fans

表示投保的险别，用 insurance against+所投保的货物，如 insurance against FPA

表示投保的保险公司，用 insurance with+所投保的保险公司，如 insurance with PICC

表示投保的金额，用 insurance for+所投保的金额，如 insurance for 110% of the invoice value

表示投保的费率，用 insurance at+所投保的费率，如 insurance at the rate of 0.5%

与 insurance 相关的短语：insurance company 保险公司，insurance agent 保险公司、保险代理人，insurance certificate 保险凭证，insurance policy 保险单，insurance coverage 保险范围，insurance amount 保险金额，insurance value 保险价

值，insurance premium 保险费，insurance industry 保险产业

We want broader coverage to include some extraneous risks.

我们要较广泛的保险，包括一些附加险。

3. cover n. 保险 v. 保险，投保

We have arranged the necessary insurance cover.

我们已经安排了必要的保险。

We shall cover the goods against All Risks.

我们将对此货物投保一切险。

coverable a. 可投保的，可承保的

Please let us know the premium at which breakage is coverable by the insurers on your side.

请告知贵处保险商承保破碎险的保费。

4. on condition that... 以……为条件

Buyer's request for insurance to be covered up to the inland city can be accepted on condition that such extra premiums are for the buyer's account.

买方所提的将保险范围延伸至内陆城市的要求可以被接受，条件是由此所引起的额外保费由买方承担。

They expressed their desire to enter into business relations with us on condition that we would allow them a standing credit of USD 5,000 to start business.

他们表达了他们愿意与我们建立业务关系的愿望，条件是我们要给予他们作为启动业务所需的 5,000 美元长期信贷。

5. invoice value 发票金额/价值

At your request, we have insured your goods for 130% of the invoice value against All Risks, but the premium difference between 110% and 130% will be borne by you.

按贵方要求，我方按发票金额的 130%投保了一切险，但 110%和 130%之间的保费差额由贵方承担。

6. at your end 贵方所在地

Our products will find a good market at your end.

我们的产品能在贵处打开销路。

Since the diplomatic relationship between our two countries was established, considerable business has been done with other buyers at your end.

自从两国建交以来,我们与贵国其他买主做了大量生意。

7. refund the premium to you 将保险费退还贵方,偿还保险费

refund n./v. 退款,偿还

As we have not received your L/C up to now, we have to cancel the contract and therefore ask you to refund us the storage charges we have paid on your behalf.

由于到目前为止我们尚未收到贵方的信用证,我们不得不取消合同并要求贵方退还我们代贵方所交的仓储费。

Consumers have the right to return faulty goods and demand a refund from the supplier.

客户有权退还瑕疵品并要求供货商退还款项。

8. premium n. 保险费,较高价格

The premium is calculated according to the premium rate or rates for risks to be covered.

保险费根据所投保的保险费率计算。

This risk is coverable at a premium of 1%.

这种险的保费是1%。

During Christmas, these commodities are selling at a premium.

圣诞节期间,这些商品按高价出售。

9. policy n. 保险单

类似的表述有:insurance policy 保险单,open policy 预约保单,voyage policy 航程保单,transferable policy 可转让的保单

10. debit note 索款通知单,借方通知书

credit note 贷方通知单

debit n. 借方 v. 将……记入借方

We have debited the amount plus our charges to your account.

我行已将该笔款项连同我行的服务费计入贵公司的借方。

11. for one's account 由某方付费,记入某方账户

We may cover insurance on your behalf, but we have to point out that the extra premium will be for your account.

我们可以代贵方投保,但必须指出额外的保费由贵方承担。

Useful Sentences 常用句型

1. We leave the insurance arrangements to you but we wish to have the goods covered against All Risks.

我们将保险留给贵方办理,但我们希望为货物投保一切险。

2. Please quote your lowest All Risks rate for shipments from Shanghai to Boston.

请报上货物从上海到波士顿投保一切险的最低费率。

3. As requested, we have covered insurance for the shipment against FPA and TPND for the invoice cost plus 20% up to the port of destination.

按照要求,我们已为货物投保平安险和偷窃、提货不着险,保险金额为发票金额加 20%,保险范围一直到目的港为止。

4. Since the premium varies with the extent of insurance, extra premium is for the buyer's account, should additional risks be covered.

保险费与保险范围相关,如果要投保额外的险别,额外的保险费由买方负担。

5. Breakage is a special risk, for which an extra premium will have to be charged.

破碎险是一种附加的险别,需收取额外的保险费。

6. We shall of course refund the premium to you upon receipt of your debit note.

当然,收到贵方的还款通知后,我们将立即退还保险费。

7. Please see to it that the above mentioned goods should be shipped before the 20th May and that shipment should be covered for 130% of the invoice value against All Risks.

请注意上述货物必须在 5 月 20 日前装运并且应为货物投保一切险,保险金额为发票金额的 130%。

8. An insurance claim should be submitted to the insurance company or its agents within 30 days after the arrival of the consignment at the port of destination.

保险索赔应在货物到达目的港30天内提交给保险公司或其代理人。

9. The cargo is to be insured as per warehouse-to-warehouse clauses.

货物将按“仓至仓”条款投保。

10. In the absence of definite instruction from our clients, we generally cover insurance against WPA and War Risks; if you desire to cover FPA, please let us know in advance.

在没有客户明确的指示前,我们一般为货物投保水渍险和战争险;如果贵方想投保平安险,请事先告知。

Exercises 练习

Ⅰ. Fill in the blanks with the appropriate words.

Dear Sirs,

____ a result of our recent exchange of e-mails ____ us, we confirm having booked your Order No. 564 ____ 400 bales ____ Cotton Piece Goods ____ CIF terms.

We wish to draw your attention ____ the fact that insurance is generally to be covered by us ____ WPA ____ 110% of the invoice value. If any other risks are to be insured ____, please let us know ____ the end of this week, so that we can adjust our insurance charges ____ and ____ shipment ____ delay. If higher percentage is required, we can do as requested ____ you bear the extra premium.

Your prompt reply will be highly appreciated.

Sincerely yours,

Ⅱ. Translate the following sentences into Chinese.

1. We hope you will cover insurance on our behalf for the consignment mentioned above.

2. For transactions concluded on FOB basis, insurance is to be covered by the Buyers.

3. We shall be pleased to know whether you can undertake insurance on wine against All Risks.

4. In the absence of your definite instructions, we cover insurance on your order as usual.

5. We will get an insurance policy as soon as we are through with all the formalities.

6. We note that you wish us to insure shipments to you for 10% above the invoice value, which is having our due attention.

7. Would you please tell us whether you can cover All Risks for the consignments and, if so, on what terms?

8. Please send the policy along with one certified copy not later than the 24th of this month, and charge the cost to the account of our branch office in Qingdao.

9. Generally we cover insurance against FPA and War Risk in the absence of definite instructions from our clients.

10. We will follow our contract and adhere to our usual practice and sincerely hope that this will not affect our future business relations.

Ⅲ. Translate the following sentences into English.

1. 我们将为 100 公吨羊毛按发票上价格的 110%投保一切险。

2. 请注意保险仅包括平安险和破碎险。如需加保其他险种,额外保费将由贵方自行负担。

3. 请注明保险只包括水渍险,按照“仓至仓”条款,有效期 15 天。

4. 货物保险应按我方到岸价格的 110%投保。如需加保其他险别,请事先通知我方,并且由买方承担所有额外费用。

5. 请按照我们的要求办理保险,同时,我们等候贵方的装运通知。

6. 破碎险的保险费率为 5%,如果贵方愿意投保破碎险,我们可以代为办理。

7. 我们可以接受贵方要求,将货物投保到内陆城市,但其额外保费须由贵方负担。

8. 保险费根据商品性质、所要投保的范围以及目的地而有所不同。

9. 如果贵方有任何关于保险方面的问题,请立即和我方联系,我方将不遗余力地为贵方服务。

10. 为安全起见,我方建议贵方为此批货物投保水渍险和战争险。

Ⅳ. Translate the following letter into Chinese.

Dear Sirs,

We refer to the 4,000 cases of iron nails under Sales Contract No. 214 and are pleased to inform you that we have established with the Bank of China, New York Branch the confirmed, irrevocable L/C No. 213 in the amount of USD 20,000, valid up to May 15.

Please see to it that the above-mentioned goods are to be shipped before May 15 and the insurance is covered for 130% of the invoice value against All Risks. As we understand that as per your customary practice, you only insure the shipment for 10% above the invoice value, and the extra premium for additional coverage shall be for our account.

Please arrange insurance according to our request and meanwhile we are expecting your shipping advice.

Yours faithfully,

Ⅴ. Translate the following letter into English.

敬启者:

兹答复贵方9月4日关于保险的来信。

贵方客户就保险范围延伸到内地城市的要求是可以接受的,条件是额外的保险费由客户支付。

此外,我们不能同意贵方的保险金额为发票金额的150%,因为合同规定要按发票金额的110%投保。

我们相信上述的信息能合贵方的意,同时我们静候佳音。

谨上

Ⅵ. Letter writing.

Write a letter to ABC Company, asking them to insure the goods as per the contract. Meanwhile please state the insurance amount and the coverage.

Further Reading
扩展阅读

Letter 7: Insurance Instruction

Dear Sirs:

Re: Insurance on Order No. 563

As a result of our recent exchange of e-mails between us, we confirm having booked your Order No. 563 for 400 bales of Cotton Piece Goods on CIF terms.

We wish to draw your attention to the fact that insurance is generally to be covered by us against WPA for 110% of the insurance value. If any other risks are to be insured against, please let us know by the end of this week, so that we can adjust our insurance charges accordingly and effect shipment without delay. If higher percentage is required, we can do as requested provided you bear the extra premium.

Your prompt reply will be highly appreciated.

Yours sincerely,

Letter 8: Insurance Instruction

Dear Sirs:

We refer to your L/C No. 158 covering Galzed Wall Tiles, which we have just received.

Please note for this article we do not cover Breakage. You have to, therefore, delete the word "Breakage" from the insurance clause in the credit.

Furthermore, we wish to point out that for such articles as window glass, porcelains, etc., even if additional Risk of Breakage has been insured, the cover is subject to a franchise of 5%. In other words, if the breakage is surveyed to be less than 5%, no claims for damage will be entertained.

We trust that the position is now clear. Please cable the amendment at once.

Yours faithfully,

Letter 9: Endorsement to an Insurance Policy

Dear Sirs,

Re: Endorsement to Our Insurance Policy No. 112

We have received your letter of July 12 in which you asked for an extension of the above policy for a period of 30 days to cover the risk of fire while the goods are laying in Customs warehouse in Hamburg.

In compliance with your request, we have issued our Endorsement No. AA134 to this effect together with the relevant debit note for an additional premium of USD $ 100. 00 and are enclosing herewith the same which we hope you will find in order.

Yours faithfully,

Encl.

Tips

Fundamental Principles of Cargo Insurance

The three fundamental principles of insurance are insurable interest, good faith and indemnity.

Insurable interest refers to the legal right to enter into an insurance contract. A person is said to have an insurable interest if the event insured against could cause that person a financial loss. For example, anyone may insure his own property as he would incur a loss if an item was lost, destroyed or damaged. If no financial loss would occur, no insurance can be arranged. For example, a person cannot insure a neighbor's property. The limit of an insurable interest is the value of the item concerned. Without an insurable interest, an insured is unable to enforce an insurance contract as it distinguishes insurance from a bet or wager.

In a contract of cargo insurance, the utmost good faith must be observed by both the assured and the insurer. If either party fails to observe good faith, the other may avoid the contract. Breach of good faith may consist of either material misrepresentation, or of non-disclosure of a material fact. Hence it is the duty of the assured to disclose to the insurer all material circumstances that are known to the assured before the contract is concluded. The material circumstance will influence the decision of the insurer as to whether or not and under what terms to accept the risk.

A cargo insurance policy is basically a contract of indemnity, an agreement to reimburse another individual or legal entity who incurs a loss covered by the agreement. An indemnity against loss may be partial or whole. A buyer may obtain indemnity insurance, for example, to insure against damage to or destruction of goods that may occur after title has been passed to the buyer.

Chapter 12 Complaints, Claims and Settlements
申诉、索赔与理赔

Learning Objectives

- Learn the definition and types of complaint and claim
- Master the contents and the types in letters about complaints and claims

学习目标:了解索赔与理赔的定义与类型;掌握索赔与理赔信件的写作内容与类型。

Case Study

After Mulberry Silk Textiles under Contract No. 001234567 reached Marseille, FG found that partial goods were not in agreement with the specifications stated in the contract. How to settle the matter? What should FG do?

Introduction

Mistakes may occur in day-to-day business, and these can cause complaints or claims. Claims refer to the situation where the injured party claims for compensation for losses in case the contract is breached. Sometimes the party suffering the loss may write a letter of complaint or make a call to attract the other party's attention to avoid this matter happening again instead of lodging a claim.

Claims or complaints may be lodged about the quantity delivered, insufficient packing, inferior quality, a discrepancy between the goods and the samples or the delay in shipment. If a complaint or claim is made by the buyer, the matter should be investigated in detail.

In a complaint or claim letter, the writer should state the complaint or claim with regret, mention the date of the order, the date of delivery, the goods complained about, the exact details of damage, breakage or loss, etc. Then he should explain the reason of his complaint, provide evidence of damage or loss and ask for an explanation. At last, he should state what he wants to be done, such as a reduction in price.

A reply to a complaint or claim should always be courteous even if the complaint or claim is unreasonable. In such letters the writer should express regret for receiving the complaint or claim letter and state what he will do to settle the matter or agree to the settlement.

Specimen Letters
样信

Letter 1: Complaint about Inferior Quality

Dear Sirs,

Re: Our Contract No. 001234567

We have received 20,000 pieces of mulberry silk textiles under our contract No. 001234567 ex S. S. Peace. Much to our regret, when the goods were **reinspected** at the port of destination, we found that the goods were not in conformity with the specification stated in the contract. The material seems to be of inferior quality.

To enable you to compare the goods delivered with the specification, we have sent you a piece of the textiles under separate cover. As inferior quality of the goods causes us considerable difficulty in marketing, we expect your opinion on how to do with it.

We are looking forward to your early reply.

Yours faithfully,

Letter 2: Reply to the Buyer's Complaint for Inferior Quality

Dear Sirs,

We have received your letter dated August 4th in which you **lodged a claim** against us on the goods under your order No. 123.

Compared the goods delivered with our original sample, we desire to inform you that the goods delivered should be similar to the sample according to the contract instead of **being identical to the sample**. Therefore the complaint is **impractical**.

We hope that our opinion is acceptable to you.

Yours sincerely,

Letter 3: Complaint for Short Weight

Dear Sirs,

Re: Our Order No. 234 for 2,000 Sets of Air Conditioners

We regret to inform you that the captioned goods unloaded here yesterday were short-weight 200 sets according to the **Survey Report** from **Shanghai Commodity Inspection Bureau**. It also evidences that the suppliers should be definitely responsible for such short weight. Therefore we lodge a claim against you for US $ 45,000.

Enclosed please find the Survey Report No. 134 and we are looking forward to your settlement at an early date.

Yours faithfully,

Encl.

Letter 4: Complaint for Poor Packing

Dear Sirs,

The air conditioners you shipped by S. S. Peace on 23rd May arrived here yesterday.

On examination, we found that some of the goods were seriously damaged. An inspection made by the surveyor showed that the damage was attributable to improper packing. For more particulars, we refer you to the surveyor's report attached.

We are therefore compelled to claim on you to compensate us for the loss, US $ 30,000.

We trust you will find the above acceptable and **deduct** the sum claimed from the amount in our next order.

Yours truly,

Encl.

Letter 5: Reply to a Complaint for Poor Packing

Dear Sirs,

We have received your letter of 4th June together with your surveyor's report, in which you informed us that the air conditioners we shipped to you arrived in a damaged condition for our poor packing.

Upon receipt of your letter, we studied your surveyor's report carefully. We find that the stated damage was due to extraordinary circumstances in transit instead of our poor packing. Therefore we are not responsible for the damage. For your information, the damage caused in transit should be responsible by the shipping company.

We hope that the above is acceptable to you.

Yours truly,

Letter 6: Reply to a Complaint for Poor Packing

Dear Sirs,

We are very sorry to learn from your letter of 4th June that the air conditioners ordered reached you in a damaged condition.

After studying your surveyor's report, we agree to your suggestion and deduct US $ 30,000 from the amount of our next invoice.

To avoid future inconvenience, we are now seeking a better packing method which can improve our packing. We assure you of the safe delivery of your orders in future.

Yours sincerely,

Words & Phrases 词汇

1. complaint n. 抱怨,申诉,投诉

make/lodge/file a complaint against sb. for sth. 因某事而向某人表示抱怨

Such being the case, we have to lodge a complaint against you for poor quality.

既然如此,我们只能就质量低劣问题向贵方提起申诉。

complain v. 申诉,抱怨

complain to sb. of/about sth. 因某事而向某人表示不满、抱怨

The buyers complained to the seller of the excessive moisture contained in the minerals.

买方因矿石中水分含量过高向卖方抱怨。

Our customers complained that the goods had been short-weighted.

我们客户抱怨货物短量。

2. re-inspect 复验

类似的表述有:re-export 复出口

3. lodge a claim 提出索赔

claim

n. 索赔,索款

make/register/file/lodge/raise/bring up a claim 提出索赔

make a claim against/with sb. 向某方提出索赔

make a claim on/for sth. 就某事提出索赔

We have lodged a claim on the goods against the Seller for US $ 30,000 for short weight.

我们就短量问题向卖方提起索赔，索赔金额为 3 万美元。

We, therefore, suggest that you lodge a claim against the shipping company for compensation.

因此，我们建议贵公司向航运公司提出索赔。

v. 索赔

The buyer claimed against us for our poor packing.

买方因低劣的包装而向我们提出索赔。

4. being identical to the sample 和样品一样

5. impractical a. 不实际的

The price quoted in your letter is impractical.

贵方信中所报价格不切实际。

6. short weight 短重

类似的表述有：short delivery 短交，short-delivered 短交，short shipment 短装，short shipped 短装，short-landed 短卸，short-paid 少付

7. Survey Report 检验报告

Survey Report on Quality 品质鉴定证明

Survey Report on Weight 重量鉴定证明

Survey Report on Examination of Damage or Shortage 检验残损证明书

8. Shanghai Commodity Inspection Bureau 上海商品检验局

9. deduct v. 扣除，减去

We will deduct the premium from your commission of 5% payable to you.

我们将从应支付给贵方 5%的佣金中扣除保险费。

Useful Sentences 常用句型

1. These cases were found to be badly damaged. This was apparently attributable to faulty packing.

这些箱子被发现严重受损。这很显然是由于包装不良引起的。

2. Your shipment of our Order No. 222 has been found short-weight by 1,000 kg, for which we must file a claim amounting to US $ 987 plus inspection fee.

贵方所装运的我们第 222 号订单货物已被发现短重 1 000 公斤，对此我们必须提起索赔，包括商检费，索赔金额为 987 美元。

3. The quality of your shipment for our order No. 234 has been found not in conformity with the agreed specification. We must therefore lodge a claim against you for the amount of US $ 998. The SCIB's survey report is forwarded herewith and your early settlement is requested.

我们第 234 号订单货物的品质被发现与协议的规格不符。因此我们必须向贵方提起索赔，金额为 998 美元。随附商检局的检验报告，并期待贵方早日处理。

4. We have to inform you that the goods we ordered from you on 12 August have not arrived yet and we have not heard anything from you concerning the shipment.

要告知贵方，我们 8 月 12 日向贵方订购的货物还没有到达此地，此外也没有收到贵方关于装运的任何信息。

5. In view of our friendly business relations, we are prepared to meet your claim for the 32 metric tons short-weight.

鉴于我们之间的友好业务关系，我们准备接受贵方提出的短重 32 公吨的索赔要求。

6. Such a claim as this without any foundation cannot be considered.

诸如这样无依据的索赔将不予考虑。

7. We regret to tell you that your claim cannot be entertained as it is raised far beyond the time limit stipulated in the contract.

我们很遗憾地告诉贵方，贵方的请求无法被受理，因为它未能在合同规定的时限内提出。

8. We wish to settle this dispute fairly, so we suggest that we submit it for arbitration.

我们希望能公平地解决争端，所以我们建议将争端提交仲裁解决。

9. In addition to the indemnification for the price difference due to the quality,

the relevant commodity inspection charges must be as well for your account.

除了赔偿因品质导致的差价外,相关的商品检验费也必须由贵方支付。

10. In checking the contents against your enclosed invoice, it was found that several items were missing.

在按照随附发票检查贵方货物时,有几件商品被发现缺失。

11. Disputes may be submitted for arbitration in case no settlement can be reached through negotiation between both parties.

如果双方之间的争议无法通过协商解决,可将它提交仲裁解决。

12. Any claim in respect of this consignment must be raised within 60 days after its arrival at the port of destination, after which no claim will be entertained.

关于货物的任何索赔必须在货到目的港 60 天内提出,此日期之后将不再考虑受理。

13. The certificate of quality issued by the official organization has already been sent to you after shipment, and it is the proof that the quality of the goods was up to standards upon shipping. As a result, we will have to decline your claim with regret.

官方机构所出具的质量证书已在装船后发送给贵方,它是货物在装运时品质达到标准的证明。因此,我们将不得不谢绝贵方的索赔要求。

14. We lodge a claim against you for the compensation, totaling US $ 2,000, for the extra cost of repacking and the shortage in weight caused by the serious leakage. Please refer to the attached copy of the survey report for detailed information about the damage.

我们向贵方提出索赔,索赔总额为 2 000 美元,包括因严重渗漏而导致的再包装的额外费用和短量。请参阅随附的有关此损害详情的调查报告副本。

Exercise 练习

Ⅰ. Translate the following sentences into Chinese.

1. Owing to your excessive delay in delivery, we notify you of our cancellation of the contract.

2. Since we have very good relations with you, we are willing to accept the shipment if you will allow a 20% reduction in price.

3. We regret to have to complain about the late delivery of the goods ordered on May 12 because, as you know, punctual shipment is of vital importance to us.

4. We acknowledge your claim and apologize for the inconvenience caused to you. Replacements of the faulty articles will be sent to you next week.

5. The goods delivered are not up to the standard of samples. The pattern is uneven in places and the coloring various.

6. The inferior quality of the goods causes us considerable difficulty and it is hard for us to dispose of them.

7. Unfortunately upon opening the case we found it contained completely different articles. We presume that a mistake was made and the contents of the case were for another order.

8. We regret to inform you that the color deviation existing between the products and the samples is normal and permissible; therefore, the compensation claimed is impracticable.

9. In view of the high quality of the article, we regret that we cannot reduce the price. If you are unable to accept it, we will make arrangements for its payment on collection.

10. We can hardly be expected to accept your claim after a lapse of over two months.

Ⅱ. Translate the Following Sentences into English.

1. 我们提出合同价格减去30%是公平合理的,否则,按照合同规定办事,买方有权退货并提出索赔。

2. 经检验,我们发现虽然箱子本身并无损坏迹象,但很多货物已严重损坏。

3. 该批货物的质量与合同规定严重不符,很遗憾我们不得不要求退货。

4. 很明显货损是由不当包装造成的,在向我方客户供货之前,我们不得不重新包装。兹向贵方提出索赔以补偿由此而产生的额外费用。

5. 这种产品与样品之间的偏差在正常的允许范围内,因此,贵方索赔将不予受理。

6. 该货从公司仓库运出时完好无损，所出现的损伤显然是在运输途中造成的。

7. 显而易见，损坏是由于粗暴装卸所致，贵方应向有关的保险公司索赔。

8. 我们正在按贵方要求改进包装，期待下批货物能达到贵方要求。

9. 这是我们所能做的最大让步，如果贵方不同意我们的提议，我们想提交仲裁解决。

10. 由于贵方提出的异议与我方试验的结果不一致，因此要求贵方做另一次检查，以便证明是否有理由提出索赔。

Ⅲ. Translate the following letter into Chinese.

Dear Sirs,

Thank you for informing us about the damage to our shipment (Invoice No. 678) of your order.

From our previous transactions you will find that this sort of problem is quite unusual. Nevertheless, we would apologize for the inconvenience it has caused you.

Would you please return the whole consignment to us, and we will ask the shipping company to inspect the damage so that they can arrange compensation. It is unlikely that our insurance company needs to be troubled with this case.

If you want us to send you another shipment as per your order No. 456, please let us know. We have the garments in stock and would be able to effect shipment within two weeks.

Yours sincerely,

Ⅳ. Translate the following letter into English.

敬启者：

事由：订单号码 No. 234

今就我公司昨日收到的露营帐篷装运不当一事向贵方提出申诉。该批帐篷是根据上列订单订购的。

装帐篷的箱子受到损坏，似乎在运输过程中已被打开。根据贵方第 678 号发票,我们估计有20件帐篷及若干照明附件被盗,价值3 200美元。由于箱子被翻乱,箱内物品已经起皱或沾上污迹,无法作为新商品在我处出售。

由于是按到岸价订货的,而且负责运货的是贵方代理,我们建议贵方就赔偿事宜与他们联系。随信附上受损失和丢失的帐篷清单。在收到贵方的复信前,该批货物将暂时另行存放。

谨上

V. Letter writing.

Write a letter of claim for inferior quality and ask for a reduction of 4% of the invoice value.

Further Reading

扩展阅读

Letter 7: Claim on Wrong Goods

Dear Sirs,

We duly received the concerned shipping documents and took delivery of the goods ex S. S. Peace yesterday.

We thank you for your prompt execution of the order. However, when we opened the cases, we found they contained completely different articles. We can only presume that the articles were for another order.

As we need our order urgently, we must ask you to arrange for the dispatch of our order at once. We enclose hereof our order for your reference.

In the meantime, we are holding the above goods at your disposal and awaiting your instruction on how to do with it.

Yours faithfully,

Encl.

Letter 8: Complaint for Breakage of the Goods

Dear Sirs,

We are writing to inform you that the toys for our Order No. 36 arrived in such an unsatisfactory condition that we have to lodge a claim against you.

It was found upon examination that 10% of the toys were broken and some are badly scratched, obviously due to the improper packing. Therefore, we cannot offer for sale at the normal price and suggest that you make us an allowance of 20% on the invoice value.

If you cannot accept, we are afraid we shall have to return them for replacement.

Yours faithfully,

Letter 9: Insurance Claim on Chinese Tea Set

Dear Sirs,

Re: Claim on Chinese Tea Set under Policy No. 112

We are holders of Policy No. 112 issued by your company, Shanghai branch on 1,000 pieces of Chinese Tea Set valued at USD 11,000. The ship encountered an accident of clash and 200 pieces of Tea Set were severely damaged. We hereby file a detailed claim for USD 4,400.00.

We are enclosing the survey report issued by the Johnson Survey Co., together with the policy No. 112, which is against All Risks.

Your prompt attention is appreciated.

Yours sincerely,

Encl.

Tips

Force Majeure

Force Majeure, also called Act of God, is an event that can be neither anticipated nor reduced to control, e. g. , an industrial strike that leads to loss of profits, or a war destroying a whole cargo, or some others of the kind.

Force majeure clause usually excuses a party who breaches the contract because the party's performance is prevented by the occurrence of an event that is beyond the party's reasonable control. A force majeure clause may excuse performance on the occurrence of such events as natural disasters like flood, storm, heavy snow, earthquake, etc. , and social disturbances like war, strike, sanctions, etc. , and performance failures outside the control of the contracting party, such as disruptions in telephone service attributable to the telephone company, labor disputes other than those of the contractual parties, government restrictions (denial or cancellation of a necessary license). A force majeure clause in the contract should specify the scope of force majeure events, consequences, time limit of notice to the other contractor, certificates required and the agencies who issue them.

There are usually two consequences of force majeure: to cancel the contract, or to postpone execution of the contract, with prior consent in the concerned contract after the occurrence of force majeure.

In case of a force majeure event, the party who quotes the clause should give prompt notice to the other party within a specified time limit. A force majeure event should also be verified by a certificate that attests such an event. The issuer of the certificate should be mentioned in the clause.

Chapter 13 Letters of Congratulations, Thanks and Invitations 祝贺信、感谢信与邀请信

Learning Objectives

- Identify situations in which letters of congratulations, thanks and invitations are written
- Apply different techniques to write the letters of congratulations, thanks and invitations

学习目标：了解何种情况下应该写祝贺信、感谢信和邀请信；掌握祝贺信、感谢信和邀请信的写作技巧。

Case Study

Mr. Anderson, has been working for ten years for FG. Recently Mr. Smith, the Marketing Director of Jin Yuan, learns that Mr. Anderson has been promoted to the International Marketing Director of the Company.

Suppose you are Mr. Smith, how should you write a letter of congratulation to Mr. Anderson?

Introduction

Every business person or organization occasionally faces circumstances which vary from the usual day-to-day operations. Many of these situations require letters that provide an opportunity to create goodwill for both the business and individual.

Every time when one feels it necessary to write a special letter, it will be an opportunity to express his or her sincere feelings about some special matters. All festival times and on such occasions as the award of an honor, a promotion, businessmen who are good at communication would take the opportunity to send their good wishes and their congratulations. Such letters are appreciated by customers and are certainly good for business because one of the most important functions of this kind of letters is to create goodwill.

Whatever the type is, such letters possess one quality in common——the quality of showing goodwill for the reader. An effective letter of thanks should contain the following: (1) state the general appreciation for what the reader has done for the writer; (2) make a sincere personal comment; (3) end with a positive and genuine statement. An effective letter of congratulations should contain the following: (1) make the reader feel certain that he or she deserves the special message of recognition and praise; (2) be brief and deal with the primary topic only; (3) carry a tone of being positive and conversational; (4) send the letter within a few days of the event.

Specimen Letters
样信

Letter 1: Congratulation from a Customer

Dear Mr. Anderson,

Allow me to convey my congratulations on your promotion to the International Managing Director. I am delighted that many years of service you have given to your organization has been recognized and appreciated.

We wish you success in your new post and look forward to closer cooperation with you in the development of business between our two companies.

Sincerely yours,

Letter 2: Congratulation from a Friend

Dear Ray,

Hearties congratulations on your promotion to chief clerk of the FG Company. I know how happy you and your family must be. You should consider this promotion as a well-deserved reward for your many years of conscientious and untiring efforts on behalf of your company.

I rejoice with you in your good fortune. My very best wishes to you as you begin your new duties.

Most Sincerely,

Letter 3: Thanks for an Offer

Dear Mr. Anderson,

I am writing to express my sincere gratitude to you for making the offer possible. I was thrilled to learn of my selection for this honor and I am deeply appreciative of your support.

I am currently majoring in Early Childhood Education with hopes of becoming an elementary teacher. The financial assistance you provided will be of great help to me in paying my educational expenses, and it will allow me to concentrate more of my time for studying.

Thank you again for your generosity and support. I promise you I will work very hard and eventually give something back to others, both as teacher and possibly a scholarship to future students like myself.

Sincerely,

Letter 4: Thanks for Introduction

Dear Mr. Bush,

This is a short note to thank you very much for introducing us to the EE Corporation. We would like to report that our visit there last month resulted in an initial order, which hopefully may develop into large orders in the future.

Without your introduction we would not have been able to establish this connection with EE, and once again we wish to thank you for your help. We look forward to expanding our relationship even further.

Yours sincerely,

Letter 5: Invitation to Attend a Fair

Dear Mr. Johnson,

We should like to invite your Corporation to attend the 2025 International Fair which will be held from August 15 to 30 at the above address. Full details on the Fair will be sent in a week.

We look forward to hearing from you soon, and hope that you will be able to attend.

Yours faithfully,

Letter 6: Invitation to Attend a Meeting

Dear WTC Colleagues,

Firstly, we would like to convey our sincere greetings from Beijing.

We are pleased to inform you that 2021 WTCA Asia – Pacific Regional Meeting(APRM 2021) will be held in Beijing during February 22–24, 2021. Commissioned by WTCA, APRM 2021 will be jointly hosted by China World Trade Center and World Trade Center Beijing.

Themed at "Connect with Worldwide WTCA Network", APRM 2021 will mainly focus on the topic of building a successful WTC, studies and best practices from Asia Pacific WTCs, WTCA networking and promotion platforms, doing business in China and etc. Meanwhile, APRM 2021 will also hold a series of round table meetings and group sessions. An exciting cultural night and new Beijing city tour will be organized for the benefit of the APRM delegates. APRM

2021 will provide a platform and an opportunity for all Asia Pacific WTCs to communicate and discuss the WTC future development in the region and the world. APRM 2021 has received the great attention from WTCA Board and HQs. Some Board Members and executives of WTCA HQs will attend the meeting to communicate and discuss together with Asia Pacific WTCs.

Hereby, we sincerely invite all the WTC colleagues from Asia Pacific and the rest of the world to take part in APRM 2021 in Beijing, to leverage this platform to strengthen communications, exchange information and thoughts, achieve mutual benefits, form extensive cooperation, and make contributions to the development of Asia Pacific WTCs.

Looking forward to meeting with you in Beijing in the spring of 2021!

Best regards,

Useful Sentences 常用句型

1. Thank you again for your wonderful hospitality and I am looking forward to seeing you soon.

再次感谢您的盛情款待，并期待不久与您会面。

2. I sincerely appreciate your generous spirit of cooperation.

对于贵方的慷慨合作精神，我真诚地致以谢意。

3. May I take this opportunity to express my hearty thanks to you.

我愿借此机会向您表示衷心的感谢。

4. Your presence is requested at the reception.

请出席招待会。

5. You are cordially invited to the dinner party.

我们诚挚地邀请您来参加晚宴。

6. Please confirm your participation at your earliest convenience.

请在您方便的时候确认能参加。

7. Congratulations and all the best wishes!

祝贺并祝福您!

8. Congratulations on your latest promotion! I know you will make good in your new job because you thrive on professionalism.

祝贺您最近的升迁！我知道您一定能胜任新的工作，因为您很专业。

9. Please accept my warmest congratulations on this 20th anniversary of the founding of your business.

请接受我对于贵公司成立二十周年衷心的祝贺。

10. It is with the greatest pleasure that I offer you sincere congratulations on your success.

对您的成功，向您致以最诚挚的祝贺。

Exercises 练习

Ⅰ. Translate the following letter into English.

亲爱的史密斯先生：

刚刚获悉您已荣升东海贸易公司总裁，在此我谨向您表示最衷心的祝贺。毫无疑问，过去的几年来，您在公司里是最辛勤工作的一个。我同大家一样非常高兴地看到，您的努力得到了回报。当然，这也是对您的能力和奉献精神的一种肯定。

我相信，这一晋升将给予您大展宏图的良好机会，我衷心祝愿您事事顺利！

谨上

Ⅱ. Translate the following letter into Chinese.

Dear Mr. Smith,

Thanks for your help in making the meeting a great success.

Your presentation was insightful that it generated a keen debate concerning the future development of the international trade. I'm certain the members have benefited greatly from your speech.

Once again, thanks again for your participating so effectively in the meeting and for playing a key role in making it a successful one.

Yours sincerely,

Further Reading

扩展阅读

Letter 7: Letter of Congratulation

Dear Mr. Smith,

As soon as I heard of your election to the board of directors of your firm, I felt I must write to you to let you know how happy I am in your advancement.

All of your friends have felt that in spite of the great difficulties you have faced in your climb up through the ranks, the outstanding ability we all recognized in you could not go unacknowledged. This advancement is certainly your due, and I think your firm should also be congratulated on taking advantage more fully of your exceptional talents.

Sincerely yours,

Letter 8: Letter of Thanks

Dear Mr. Smith,

Thank you for attending our meeting last Friday and for sharing your suggestions and experience with us. As beginners in telecommunications business, our group found your suggestions and recommendations extremely helpful.

We hope we can return the favor in the future. Just give us a call when we can assist in any way.

Sincerely yours,

Letter 9: Reply to Congratulation on Promotion

Dear Mr. Owens,

Many thanks for your nice words about my promotion and for the good wishes.

The new job is going to be demanding, especially as I make the transition. I am going to give it my all, however. Your support and contribution will help ease the burden and open up a new era in our common fields.

Again, I truly appreciate your thoughtfulness for my promotion. I am looking forward to more opportunities of working with you and wish you every success.

Cordially yours,

Letter 10: Letter of Invitation

Dear Dr Marii,

Thank you for accepting our invitation to be the guest speaker for our meeting on september 22nd 2025 at the Four Points Hotel, 123 Kings Street, Kingston, Ontario.

We look forward to your presentation on the latest developments in the area of International Shipment Tracking.

We invite you to be our guest for Lunch at 1 : 00 pm. The training seminar begins at 3 : 00 pm, with an hour and a half allocated for your presentation. There will be a question and answer period after your presentation.

Kindly let us know what types of equipment you will need for your presentation. The seminar room is equipped with a computer and a multimedia projector should you require one. Should you prefer to use your own equipment, kindly let us know as well, so that we can ensure that we are well prepared.

I will contact you the first week in September to finalize the arrangements.

Once again, thank you for agreeing to speak to us.

Dr. Andre Pastel

Program Coordinator

Tips

The Different Ways to Promote International Events

Once the target market is defined, the event planners need to promote their events to invite attendees. There are different ways to promote international events.

Promote by the event brochure. The event brochure, also called the event invitation, is the first work document sent to potential exhibiting companies so as to provide them with information concerning the event to be held and to invite them to participate in. Since the beginning of the 21st century, people have been more and more used to the Internet technology and the telecommunication, and the traditional means of sales promotion have become outdated. And the use of brochures has been even marginalized. In spite of their less important role and less frequent use, brochures still contribute to the organizational work of events. The elegantly-designed and exquisitely-printed booklets are far more official and presentable than fax and electronic versions and are still indispensable on some publicity occasions, such as press conferences, industrial annual conferences and personal visits to valuable customers.

Promote by fax. This is one of the popular means whereby salesperson sends invitations and shows materials to potential clients through the fax machine. It has the advantage of accuracy and promptness, which enjoys a point-to-point communications between the organizing companies and the potentials, but its disadvantages are also obvious. For example, it incurs high cost, enormous time, and much manpower. Nevertheless, it is still deservedly adopted in event companies in the hand-receivers of the show material are purposely targeted and also the valuable show information can be widely reached within relevant communities.

Promote by telephone. This is currently the most-often-used and effective promotion means, which aims to establish voice-to-voice communication with prospective participant, provide them with individualized services, or to maintain a long-term personal contact with each other, in order to get them in the trade show ultimately. This mode of sales promotion enjoys the advantages of leaving a favorable impression upon the clients and persuading them in joining the show by elaborating on benefits they can receive in the show. Nonetheless, it is not without weaknesses: only those who have mastered the sales call skills are up to this demanding and time-consuming task; it is more likely that they have to stand countless rejections over the phone calls day after day, and go through high-pressured and frustrating experiences, which may cause negative impact on the sales work.

Promote by e-mail. The popularization of the Internet has ushered in an era of sales promotion by electronic means. By e-mail, salespeople can send invitations and event information to clients, persuade or urge them to take part in the show, as well as provide various services throughout the period before the opening of the event. E-marketing has the advantages of surprising swiftness, practical convenience and close interaction between salespeople and clients. With the help of e-mailing, salespeople can send informative brochures, keep good track of customers and store electronic files of correspondence between them. However, it is unavoidable to bear its shortcomings, such as loss of contact due to the system breakdown, uncertainty about the clients' receiving the e-mail in due time, and the inaccuracy and informality of the electronic versions of the business documents.

Promote by personal visit. Besides the above-mentioned modes of sales promotion, some more advanced means are applied in the daily work, which include face-to-face call, sales visit at similar exhibitions or on annual conferences of trade associations, key accounts acquisition, international pavilions, group participations, etc.

All these sales promotions have come into practice along with the rapid development of the event industry. What is special about them is that salespeople attach more importance to providing individualized services to potential event participants and intensifying promotional work in related industries. The ultimate aim of the event organizers is to enhance organizers' profile, display advanced technologies, expand business channels, and satisfy the needs of professional audiences.

Key to the Exercises
练习答案

Chapter 1

Ⅰ. Arrange the following parts of a letter in the correct order and form, either in block format or in indented format.

State Insurance Corporation

345 Hightower Boulevard, Prince Town, US 12345

Tel: 03-34570000 Fax: 03-34570000

Our ref: SIC 342

May 4th, 2025

Mr. R. Jameson

25 Silverthorn Garden, BATH Somerset

BA2 9AN, Britain

Attn: Business Manager

Dear Mr. Jameson,

Subject: Filling System Catalogues

We should be grateful for these copies of your current catalogues. We are particularly interested in filing cabinets.

Yours sincerely,

David Peters

Sales Manager

DP/MJ

Enclosure: 1 pricelist

C. C. Mr. Paul Johnson

Ⅱ. Address an envelope for the above letter, either in block form or in indented form.

David Peters   stamp

Sales Manager

State Insurance Corporation

345 Hightower Boulevard, Prince Town, US 12345

Tel: 03-34570000 Fax: 03-34570000

Mr. R Jameson

25 Silverthorn Garden, BATH Somerset

BA2 9AN, Britain

Chapter 2

Ⅰ. Improve the following sentences.

1. Thank you for your L/C No. 4432.

2. We hope you will consider our proposals.

3. I warmly congratulate you on your being appointed the Managing Director, and am very pleased that your 20 years of service should have been rewarded in this way.

4. Please let us know if you have any questions.

5. We thank you for your letter of May 8th and are pleased to make you an offer as follows.

6. I will make a decision only next month.

7. Last spring, we decided in Melbourne to continue the talks at this Fair.

8. He badly needs someone to help him promote sales.

9. We are sorry to be unable to offer you the sole agency you requested.

10. If you are interested, we can arrange for a demonstration of the new machines.

11. If you want this change, we must sign and date the attached form.

12. The drawing is enclosed for your approval.

13. We are likely to suffer a loss this quarter.

14. It is your turn to acquire compensation.

15. As you are our old customer, we prepare to give you a discount of 5%.

Ⅱ. Choose the best opening or closing.

1. b 2. b 3. b 4. b

Ⅲ. Organize the following sentences into a sensible order or a natural method.

1. We are an expanding electronic supply store selling to retailers and also to ordinary customers on hire purchase terms. Our expansion is being held up at present by a lack of finance. Our hire purchase customers tend to spread payments over 2 or 3 years. Is there any way in which you can assist us with finance? What would be the terms and arrangements if we ask you to assist us?

2. We thank you for your enquiry of May 9. We are glad to say that we have found a ship which we think will serve you very well. The ship is m. v. Carnilia with a cargo capacity of about 5,000 registered tons. And for a charter of 12 months the owners are prepared to consider a special rate. The ship is now at Antwerp and can be ready to load at four or five days definite notice. We will prepare the charter party and send it to you as soon as we receive you cable confirmation.

3. The store received your credit application form on time, but it was filled out incorrectly. Your form is being returned to you for proper signing. As the form indicates, your signature should be written on the bottom of both pages, but you neglected to do this.

Chapter 3

Ⅰ. Fill in the blanks with the proper word.

obtained, from, establishment, relations, contacted, main, interested, sure, at, to, appoint, reference, forward

Ⅱ. Translate the following sentences into Chinese.

1. 经纽约 ABC 公司的推荐,我们很高兴地得知贵公司的名称。

2. 我们借此机会做一自我介绍,我们是瓷质茶壶的出口商,在该行业有多年的经验。

3. 我们专业于中国轻工产品的出口,在此表达和贵方在该领域进行贸易的愿望。

4. 我们愿在平等互利的基础上和贵方建立业务联系。

5. 我们想购买化肥。

6. 我们的市场调查表明贵方对进口机器设备感兴趣。

7. 一收到贵方具体的询盘,我们将很乐意寄出报价和样品。

8. 我公司是一家从事进出口业务近 20 年的大型贸易公司,信誉良好。

9. 作为印度一家大型汽车修理连锁店,我们有 52 个对汽车配件和维修机器有强烈需求的基地。

10. 我们了解到贵方是中国丝绸产品潜在的买方,这在我们的业务范围内。

Ⅲ. Translate the following sentences into English.

1. Being one of the major importers of Japanese silk product, we are writing to you in the hope that we can enter into direct business relations with you.

2. Export of toys falls within the scope of our business activities.

3. We learn from our Commercial Council's Office in France that you are interested in electric appliance manufactured in China.

4. As we specialize in export of light industrial products, we desire to trade with you in this line.

5. To give you a general idea of our products, we are sending you a catalogue under separate cover for your reference.

6. We avail ourselves of this opportunity to write to you and wonder whether we can establish business relationship with you.

7. We should be grateful if you can inform us whether you are interested in the above business.

8. We have the pleasure to introduce ourselves to you hoping to cooperate with

you and expand business.

9. We are well connected in the circle and have experience in handling import and export of such products.

10. Our products are well accepted all over the world and we believe there is a great market potential in your country.

Ⅳ. Translate the following letter into Chinese.

敬启者:

从我们多伦多办事处发来的电子邮件中,我们了解到贵方是多伦多拥有良好资信、可信赖的公司之一,并且对不同纸张的出口尤其感兴趣。

我们借此信件和贵方联系,希望能和贵方建立业务关系并能尽快收到贵方的商品目录和其他的印刷品以供参考。

近年来,我们和贵地区最大、最知名的公司做了很多业务。正如您所知,此地进口国外产品的可能性很大,尤其是我们正在大力发展经济。

我们相信,如果贵方能在货物装运、价格和品质方面和我们合作,我们能够和贵方签下大订单。

期待不久能和贵方建立友好的业务关系。

谨上

Ⅴ. Translate the following letter into English.

Dear Sirs,

We have your name and address from our Chamber of Commerce here and are now writing to you for establishing business relations with you.

We are one of the largest importers of chemicals in Guangzhou and well connected with all the major wholesalers and retailers here. Therefore, we are sure that we can sell large quantities of your goods if you can make us offers at competitive price besides prompt delivery.

Please let us have all the necessary information regarding your products for export.

Yours sincerely,

Ⅵ. Letter writing.

Dear Sirs,

Through the courtesy of our Commercial Counselor ' s Office in London, we notice that you are interested in doing business with us.

Our lines are mainly textiles. We wish to establish business relations by the commencement of some practical transactions. To give you a general idea of the various kinds of textiles now available for export, we are enclosing herewith a catalogue and a price list for your information. We would appreciate receiving your specific enquiries.

As to our financial standing, please refer to our banker, Bank of China, London Branch.

We look forward to receiving your favorable reply.

Yours faithfully,

Chapter 4

Ⅰ. Fill in the blanks with the proper word.

from, handle, leading, large, enjoy, near, send, together, terms, helpful, send, of

Ⅱ. Translate the following sentences into Chinese.

1. 如果贵方能提供我们所询产品,我们可能会定期大量订货。

2. 报价时,请说明付款方式和可允许的数量折扣,因为我们一般大量订货。

3. 如果贵方能寄给我们最新的样品及最好报价,我们将不胜感激。

4. 为了让贵方对我们经营的电子产品有所了解,我们将另邮几份商品简介供贵方参考。

5. 如果贵方能航邮给我们当前可供出口的商品目录和价目单,我们将非常感谢。

6. 我们是纺织品的大经销商,我们相信所提商品若价格适中在我们这儿是会有市场潜力的。

7. 在答复时,请说明付款方式及在每件商品订货数量不低于 50 打时的购货折扣。

8. 我们现在愿意从贵公司购货,因为我们了解到贵公司能以更具吸引力的价格大量供货。

9. 在答复时,要求贵方报下述商品的最低价。

10. 我们和此地主要轻工产品的经销商关系很好并相信如果贵方报价具有竞争力，我们将大量销售中国产品。

Ⅲ. Translate the following sentences into English.

1. We are interested in your blouses. Please inform us whether you can supply from stock.

2. Please inform us whether you can grant 3% discount for orders above 100 metric tons.

3. We are in the market for washing machines. Please send us your catalogue with a pricelist for our reference.

4. Please inform us in detail of the major products you handle and the terms and conditions.

5. We intend to import your products. We shall be grateful if you can mail us a catalogue, samples and a pricelist.

6. We are sure you will give attention to this enquiry and give us an early reply.

7. We would appreciate it if you will let us know the ruling price of the goods.

8. Please supply a sample of your lately rayon handkerchief which accords with the sample sent herewith in terms of pattern and quality.

9. As there is a growing demand for such equipment, we have to ask for a special discount.

10. If this first order is executed to our satisfaction, we shall place repeat orders with you.

Ⅳ. Translate the following letter into Chinese.

敬启者：

我们对贵方在最新一期《办公设备》杂志中所做的新文件柜广告很感兴趣，想要获取一些更多的信息。

目前我们使用的是抽屉式的文件柜，我们想了解以下信息：

1. 新系统是否更容易、更快捷操作？

2. 每个柜子里能放置多少个文件夹？

3. 每个文件夹的容量多大？

我们现在的办公家具是浅灰色的，我们希望能尽可能地匹配。能否让我们看看有可能提供的颜色的样本？

由于我们正在重新计划全公司的办公系统，如果能收到贵方快速的答复，我们将不胜感激。

谨上

Ⅴ. Translate the following letter into English.

Dear Sirs,

Subject: Newspaper Printing Machine Type No. KG121

Referring to our business negotiation during the East-China Fair held last month in Shanghai, we would like to enquire whether you can now make us a firm offer for 200 sets of Newspaper Printing Machine Type No. KG121 on the basis of CIF Boston.

As our customers are badly in need of this type of machine, it will be greatly appreciated if you can give this enquiry your prompt attention.

Yours faithfully,

Ⅵ. Letter writing.

Dear Sirs,

We learn from the Chamber of Commerce of China, Beijing that you are producing for export kitchen wares. There is a steady demand here for kitchen wares of high quality.

Will you please send us a copy of your catalogue, a quotation with details of discount you can allow on quantities over 2,000 pieces and terms of payment? We should be grateful if you could also supply samples of the various kitchen wares.

Yours sincerely,

Chapter 5

Ⅰ. Fill in the blanks with the appropriate words.

of, in, position, for, on, by, prior, within, after, forward, open

Ⅱ. Translate the following sentences into Chinese.

1. 根据贵方的要求，我们现报盘如下，以我方最后确认为准。
2. 请注意该报盘在本月 12 日前接受有效。

3. 我们相信贵方能接受我们的报盘,该报盘只对电报回复有效。

4. 我们很高兴收到贵方6月4日询盘,现确认今早电报报盘,内容如下。

5. 市场有一上升坚挺势头,我们从贵方利益考虑建议贵方接受我们的报价。

6. 我们没有木材的现货,很遗憾不能给贵方报盘。

7. 除非另有说明,所有的价格都是不含佣金的净价。

8. 如果贵方的订货超过2 000套,我们打算报一特别价格,每套10美元,3%的折扣。

9. 我们对该商品的报价为每盒10美元,FOB上海。

10. 由于报价前所未有的低并很可能会上升,我们建议贵方立即接受我们的报盘。

Ⅲ. Translate the following sentences into English.

1. As to the product for the newest model mentioned, we are pleased to quote you as follows.

2. As requested we are offering firm for 50 metric tons of beans as follows subject to your reply here within a week from the date of writing.

3. If you find this offer acceptable, please cable us for our confirmation.

4. These quotations are all subject to the fluctuation of the market.

5. We can offer you for various kinds of Chinese cotton at attractive prices.

6. We are now in reply to your enquiry of Oct. 2nd and offer for 5 metric tons of walnut meat CFR Hamburg.

7. We hope you will consider our price competitive as our clothes are of fine quality.

8. We have pleasure of enclosing a copy of our current quotation for your reference. We can supply the goods from stock and hope to receive your order by cable soon.

9. We are an exporter of household appliances and take the liberty of sending you our quotation for your choice.

10. We understand that there is a strong demand for sportswear in your market. So we take the opportunity of enclosing our quotation No. 21 for your consideration.

Ⅳ. Translate the following letter into Chinese.

敬启者：

很高兴收到您 5 月 28 日有关优质彩色电视机的询盘。目前，我们新机型采用最先进的技术，并保证 3 年内免费更换零件。贵方对此一定会感兴趣。

我们现在任务很饱满，订单已接到 8 月底。我们每月最多只能供应您 1 000 台电视机和相关零件。

随函附上我方机器出口价格及付款条件的详细情况。我们将另邮给贵方带有图表的商品目录。

我们十分期待与贵方达成交易。

谨上

Ⅴ. Translate the following letter into English.

Dear Sirs,

We were very pleased to receive your inquiry of August 25th and enclose our illustrated catalogue and the detailed pricelist as required. Also by separate post we are sending you some samples.

When you have examined them, we feel confident that you will find the quality of the goods to be fine and the prices to be reasonable. Because of their warmth and softness, all-cotton bedclothes are more and more popular. After studying our prices you will not be surprised to learn that we are finding it difficult to meet the demand of the market.

But if you place your order not later than September 30th, we would try to effect shipment within fourteen days on receipt of your order. On regular purchase of fifty dozen or more of individual items we would allow you a discount of 5%.

We invite your attention to our other products, details of which you will find in the catalogue and look forward to receiving your fresh order.

Yours faithfully,

Ⅵ. Letter writing.

Dear Sirs,

We have for acknowledgement your letter of 4 May and take pleasure in making you the following offer subject to your reply reaching us on or before 18 May:

Commodity: Washing Machines

Specification: XQB 38-83

Quantity: 500 sets

Price: US $ 232 per set CIF New York

Shipment: within one month after receipt of your L/C

Payment: by confirmed, irrevocable L/C payable against draft at sight in our favor for the full invoice value.

If we can be of any further help, please feel free to contact us.

Yours truly,

Chapter 6

Ⅰ. Fill in the blanks with the proper words.

in, inclusive, appreciating, made, accepted, risen, past, competitive, market, reduce, by, further, quantities, reply

Ⅱ. Translate the following sentences into Chinese.

1. 由于存货不足,很遗憾我们不能接受贵方的续订单。
2. 如果贵方能对报价做出3%的减让,贵方的价格将具有相当的竞争力。
3. 我们希望贵方能设法接受九月份装运。
4. 我们对这件商品能给予的最高折扣为10%。
5. 这是最低价,所以我们不接受任何的减让。
6. 我们愿意接受贵方将价格降低至每箱30美元的要求,但贵方的最低订货数应为100公吨。
7. 如果(价格的)大幅减让可行,我们将重新考虑贵方修订后的报价。
8. 我们非常感谢贵方给予我们报盘,但很遗憾我们当前不打算购买该商品。
9. 除非价格和商场行情一致,否则想要说服客户从贵方购货很困难。
10. 只有贵方保证改进商品的包装,我们才能够接受贵方的特殊报盘。

Ⅲ. Translate the following sentences into English.

1. We cannot accept your quotation as it leaves us little margin of profit.
2. Considering the close cooperation between us, we will meet you half way to conclude the deal with you, that is, a reduction by 5%.

3. We regret to say that it is impossible to reduce the price to 15% required.

4. It is a pity that we cannot supply the goods on the terms and conditions required by you.

5. At present such specialty goods are out of stock and cannot be manufactured immediately in the factory. Please understand that we cannot guarantee delivery within three months after receipt of the order.

6. We regret that we cannot comply with your special requirement of packing but we would like to make a special offer as follows.

7. For the limitation of our stock, the goods should be shipped in three lots. Can you accept such arrangement?

8. Thank you for your samples of cotton goods. But we are not interested in them at present.

9. As our raw materials were allocated to other orders several months ago, we cannot entertain your order at present.

10. As the market tends to be firm, we prefer you to place an order as soon as possible.

Ⅳ. Translate the following letter into Chinese.

敬启者:

事由:有关贵方糖的报盘

感谢贵方2月20日的来信,信中对标题项下商品报盘:50长吨,每长吨105美元,通常条款。

作为答复,我们很遗憾地说明我们此地的最终用户认为贵方的价格太高了,和当前的市场行情不一致。资料表明,英国产的糖在此地的售价为每长吨98美元。

既然如此,我们不可能说服我们的最终用户接受贵方的价格,因为类似品质的商品可以以低得多的价格很容易地获取。如果贵方打算降低价格,比如说8%,我们可能达成交易。

正是由于考虑到我们之间的长期业务关系,我们做此还盘。由于市场是走弱的,我们希望贵方能有诚意地考虑我们的还盘,并在方便的情况下以传真方式接受。

期待贵方早日答复。

谨上

V. Translate the following letter into English.

Dear Sirs,

We are glad to have received your letter of Sep. 18th offering us Changhong Brand color TV sets inch 34 at CIF Copenhagen USD 450 per set.

In reply, we regret to inform you that your price is too high. Market information tells us that some Japanese color TV sets have been sold here at a level about 30% lower than yours.

We do not deny the quality of Changhong Brand color TV sets, but the difference in price is a wide gap. To step up the trade, we counter-offer you 10,000 Changhong Brand color TV sets inch 34 at CIF Copenhagen USD 430 per set.

It is hoped that you would seriously take it into consideration and let us have your reply very soon.

Sincerely yours,

VI. Letter writing.

Dear Sir,

We acknowledge receipt of your offer of 10 May for 500 sets of sewing machines.

While appreciating the good quality of your products, we find your price is rather too high for the market we wish to supply. We have also to point that the sewing machines available from South Korea are at prices from 15% to 20% below yours.

Such being the case, we would ask you to consider if you can make reduction in your price by 10% for the initial order. If such reduction is made, we might come to terms.

We are awaiting your acceptance by cable at your earliest convenience.

Yours faithfully,

Chapter 7

I. Translate the following sentences into Chinese.

1. 如果贵方价格和其他供货商相比有利的话,我们将向贵方订货。
2. 贵方订单受到我们密切的关注,请相信我们会在规定时间内安排装运。
3. 我们希望货物能按时到达贵方,并期待收到贵方更多的订单。
4. 由于我方客户急需此货物,我们希望贵方能早日发货。

5. 我们确认按信中所述价格给贵方供 10 000 打桌布，一收到贵方信用证就安排首班轮船装运。

6. 感谢贵方的订单，希望能在不远的将来再次给贵方供货。

7. 我们必须坚持即期交货，否则我们将被迫按照合同条款取消订单。

8. 我们发现商品质量与价格都是令人满意的，如果如下商品能够按所述价格供现货，我们将很愿意继续订货。

9. 如果所需商品无现货，请替换一个相似的商品。

10. 我们期待上述商品畅销并希望不久能更多、更大量地订货。

Ⅱ. Translate the following sentences into English.

1. Please rest assured that we shall execute your order as per the agreed terms and conditions.

2. As the goods are out of stock, we cannot accept any new orders. As soon as the new supply is available, we will contact you by cable immediately.

3. We have to stress that this is the fresh order and we will place repeat and regular orders with you if the first shipment proves to our satisfaction.

4. If you are interested in such articles, we can make an offer for the limited stock for delivery in April.

5. If you can place an order promptly, we can arrange shipment this month.

6. We shall appreciate your placing an order promptly.

7. Please supply us 50 metric tons of bitter apricot kernel as per your sample.

8. We are sorry to inform you that we have to cancel the order as our buyer does not confirm it at your price.

9. The price and the quality of your offer prove to our satisfaction. We are enclosing the following order.

10. We expect that this lot will enjoy a ready market and hope to place further orders for larger quantities with you soon.

Ⅲ. Fill in the contract forms in English with the particulars from the following messages.

Contract No. 5454

Sellers: Beijing Light Industrial Products Imp & Exp Corp.

Buyers: Boston Trading Co. , Ltd.

This Contract is made by and between the Buyers and the Sellers, whereby the Buyers agree to buy and the Sellers agree to sell the under-mentioned commodity according to the terms and conditions stipulated below:

Commodity: Fountain Pens

Specifications: Model LC001

Quantity: 1,000 dozen

Unit Price: At US $ 19 per dozen CFR Boston

Total Value: US $ 19,000 (Say US Dollars Nineteen Thousand Only)

Packing: In boxes of one dozen each, and 20 boxes to a carton

Shipping Mark: At Seller's option

Insurance: To be covered by the Buyers

Time of Shipment: During March/April 2025

Port of Shipment: China Port

Port of Destination: Boston

Terms of Payment: By confirmed, irrevocable L/C payable against draft at sight

Done and signed in Beijing on this 18th day of January, 2025.

Ⅳ. Translate the following letter into Chinese.

敬启者:

"鹦鹉"牌白水泥

作为我们最近电报往来的结果,我们确认已从贵公司购买 1 000 长吨的标题货物,条件及金额如下:

单价:成本加运费热那亚每长吨 225 欧元,净装运数量

包装:6 层牛皮纸袋,每袋净重约 110 磅

质量:根据卖方的保证,货物完全合乎中国出口标准

装运:2025 年 1 月从秦皇岛分一至两批运到热那亚,最好用直达船

支付:以贵公司为受益人保兑的、不可撤销的即期信用证

我们很高兴由于贵公司的合作达成首笔交易,并期望为了我们双方的利益进一步扩展贸易。

谨上

V. Translate the following letter into English.

Dear Sirs,

Contract No. 78PG017

We have received the captioned shipment ex S. S. East Wind and are very pleased to inform you that we find the goods quite satisfactory. As we believe we can sell additional quantities in this market, we wish to place with you a repeat order for 1,000 dozen of the same style and sizes. If possible, please arrange early shipment of this repeat order, as we are badly in need of the goods.

In case these said goods are not available from stock, we shall be very grateful to you, if you will advise us as to the specifications of those which can be shipped from stock, stating full particulars.

Yours faithfully,

VI. Letter writing.

Dear Sirs,

We have pleasure in receiving your order for wool underwear and confirm that we can supply them on the terms and conditions stated in your order. Our S/C No. AB123 in two originals is enclosed. Please countersign them and return one copy for our file.

You may rest assured that we will effect shipment without delay on receipt of your L/C. Meanwhile the order will be executed to your entire satisfaction.

We appreciate your cooperation in ordering and look forward to your further orders.

Yours sincerely,

Chapter 8

I. Translate the following sentences into Chinese.

1. 关于我方第 3232 号售货确认书的商品,我们想提请贵方注意交货期快到了,但到目前为止我们还未收到相关的信用证。

2. 对于贵方的试订单,我们打算接受付款交单的付款方式。

3. 很遗憾我们不能考虑贵方提出的承兑交单付款要求。

4. 装运单据正本已提交此地的保兑行要求付款。

5. 为避免随后修改信用证的麻烦，请注意信用证条款须和合同条款完全一致。

6. 信用证授权贵方在完成装运后可给纽约银行开立 60 天的汇票，金额为发票价值。

7. 既然没有延期付款的其他理由，我们期待贵方确认承兑我方开给贵方的 60 天汇票的传真。

8. 我们期待收到贵方银行对上述信用证展期的通知以便我们安排该货物的装运。

9. 汇票必须随附整套清洁、已装船海运提单，空白抬头、空白背书，标注“运费预付”。

10. 我们感谢贵方在报价上的合作，但我们建议贵方对付款条款做一些调整。

Ⅱ. Translate the following sentences into English.

1. As requested, we will make an exception to our rules and accept payment by D/A at 30 days.

2. We shall be grateful if you agree to make concession in payment terms, i. e. D/P at sight.

3. Please amend the L/C as follows: delete the word “long” before “ton” and insert the word “metric”.

4. You must expedite the covering L/C, otherwise we shall be unable to effect shipment before the end of this month.

5. You should open the L/C by March 2nd, 2025; otherwise we reserve the right to cancel the contract without notice.

6. We regret to inform you that we cannot accept payment by D/P in our usual practice.

7. Please attention that payment should be made by confirmed, irrevocable letter of credit with partial shipment and transshipment allowed clause, available by draft at sight.

8. We learned from your telex that the L/C was established. It is a pity that we have not received the banker’s notice. Please urge the confirming bank in London to

act as soon as possible.

9. According to the terms in the contract, payment should be made by L/C at sight instead of D/P at sight.

10. The prices for your shirts are acceptable. If you accept payment by D/P, we would like to place a trial order for 2,000 pieces.

Ⅲ. Translate the following letter into Chinese.

敬启者:

非常高兴收到贵方第 AS05 号售货确认书。我们已按要求会签并退回一份给贵方存档。

因贵方通常的付款方式是即期信用证,我们已指示我们的银行,the National Bank of Dubai Ltd.,开罗支行,开立了以贵方为受益人,金额为 600 000 欧元的相关信用证,该信用证不久将抵贵处。

请注意所供商品的品质、交货时间和售货确认书里所规定的其他条款。如果订单的执行令人满意,在不久的将来,我们将会继续订货。

谨上

Ⅳ. Translate the following letter into English.

Dear Sirs,

We would like to inform you that the goods under your Order No. 788 have been ready for shipment for quite some time, but up to now we have neither received your relevant L/C nor heard anything from you. For these, we cabled you the day before yesterday but got no reply from you either.

As you know, there is only one steamer for your port every month and the deadline for booking the shipping space on the steamer sailing this month has long been passed. Therefore, it is absolutely impossible for us to ship the goods within this month. Such being the case, we have to ask you to extend the date of shipment and the expiry date of your L/C to June 30th and July 15th, 2025 respectively.

We hope you will act promptly as requested and let us have your reply at an early date.

Yours sincerely,

V. Letter writing.

Dear Sirs,

Thank you very much for your L/C No. F-07567. However, upon checking, we have found some discrepancies and would request you to make the following amendments:

1. The place of expiry should be in China instead of Melbourne.

2. The amount both in figures and in words should respectively to be USD 150,000.00 and Say Hundred and Fifty Thousand Only.

3. Transshipment should be allowed.

4. Delete insurance clause.

5. The specifications should be tins of 450 grams instead of 500 grams.

Please make amendments as soon as possible so as to enable us to arrange shipment.

Yours faithfully,

Chapter 9

I. Translate the following sentences into Chinese.

1. 木箱不仅应适合海运,而且应足够牢固以保护货物免受损害。

2. 每 100 打包装于一个木箱中,标注上商标,然后从 1 开始编号。

3. 在外包装上请标注"小心轻放"和"冷藏"。

4. 我们必须说明不同包装材料的包装费用是不相同的。

5. 为获得更好的效果,我们现在使用塑料袋而不是纸袋包装,这不仅会给商品更好的保护,而且会增加商品的吸引力。

6. 运费成本的持续增长迫使我们改进包装方法,贵方能否为我们的产品提议更为经济的包装方式呢?

7. 我们的客户希望商品的内包装为窗式包装,以便它们能被直接看见。

8. 我们的观点是如果纸板盒包装能让我方客户满意,贵方将来可以继续这种包装方式。如果情况并非如此,我们担心这会大大影响我们之间业务的发展。

9. 关于唛头,请在包上标注我方名字首字母的缩写、目的港和以下合同号。

10. 我们在力所能及范围内尽力改进包装方式以保护商品免受破损。

Ⅱ. Translate the following sentences into English.

1. As usual a diamond should be stenciled on each case with our initials inside.

2. We would adopt packing in wooden cases instead of cartons.

3. Please pay special attention to packing; otherwise the goods will be damaged in transit.

4. Your products are of fine quality but poor inner packing which hardly attracts the customers. For our future orders, please improve packing.

5. As the goods will be transshipped, we hope that each case should be marked with the weights, warning marks, indicative marks and your own marks.

6. We are enclosing the shipping mark for our goods, which should be stenciled clearly and correctly.

7. All bales have an inner waterproof lining to protect the good.

8. Please take necessary measures to protect the goods against moisture and rain as these shirts are susceptible to damage caused by moisture or rain in transit.

9. The packing and marking shall be at the seller' s option. Generally speaking, the charges of packing shall be for the buyer's account.

10. We would suggest adopting neutral packing for this lot. Please inform us whether it is acceptable to you.

Ⅲ. Translate the following letter into Chinese.

敬启者:

5 月 20 日收到贵公司 40 个纸板箱钢螺钉。

然而,其中 10 个纸箱在运送途中损坏,令货物散落。

本公司谅解此非贵公司之过失,但希望贵公司能改进包装的方法,以避免同类事件发生。

我方要求日后的包装为木箱装,净重 20 千克,可装每个净重 500 克的纸板箱 40 个。

烦请确认上述方法,并告知新方法是否会引起价格上涨。

盼望早日赐复。

谨上

Ⅳ. Translate the following letter into English.

Dear Sirs,

Re: Sales Confirmation No. 99

We thank you for your letter dated October 10, enclosing the above Sales Contract in duplicate but wish to state that the packing clause in the contract is not clear enough. The relative clause should be read:

Packing: seaworthy export packing, suitable for long distance ocean transportation

The shirts under the captioned contract should be packed in plastic bags, five dozen to one carton, 20 cartons on a pallet, and 10 pallets in FCL container. On the outer packing please mark our initials in a triangle, under which the port of destination and our order number should be stenciled. In addition, directive marks like WATERPROOF, etc. should also be indicated.

We hope you will pay special attention to the packing and look forward to receiving your shipping advice soon.

Yours faithfully,

Ⅴ. Letter writing.

Dear Sirs,

We have pleasure of receiving your letter of April 5th enquiring about the packing and marking for our Order No. 34. As requested we wish to state as follows:

(1) Our order goods should be packed in cartons of two dozen each.

(2) In addition to the gross, net and tare weights, our initials SCC in a diamond should be stenciled under which comes the port of destination and order No. 34.

We anticipate your cooperation in executing our orders.

Yours faithfully,

Chapter 10

Ⅰ. Translate the following sentences into Chinese.

1. 我们想告知贵方第342号售货确认书下的商品已于2024年12月23日装上“和平”号，新加坡转船，预计2025年1月初到达贵方港口。

2. 最早装运期是8月。我们希望贵方客户能接受。

3. 由于购货是 FOB 价,贵方应该将货物在新加坡装上我们指派的船只。

4. 由于市场低迷,请将我方订单的装运延迟至 3 月。

5. 如果贵方希望更早装运,我们只能在 7 月装运 50 公吨的钢材,其余的 50 公吨 8 月装运。

6. 如果贵方不能在此日期前装运货物,我们将取消订单并据此要求补偿。

7. 相关信用证规定的最迟交货期为 7 月 1 日或之前,请给我们报此日期前从上海驶往纽约的船运集装箱。

8. 供贵方参考,Mermaid 号预计 7 月 15 日前后从上海驶往纽约。请告知我们贵方是否希望通过那条船只装运十箱艺术品。

9. 请为该货物预订船运集装箱并尽可能早地告知我们运费。

10. 请注意分批装运和转运是不允许的。

Ⅱ. Translate the following sentences into English.

1. The above order goods have been ready. Please give us forwarding instructions as soon as possible.

2. We have sent you the goods ordered last week and hope you will find same satisfactory.

3. As per the contract, the seller should cable the shipping advice as soon as the goods are shipped on board.

4. We will book shipping space of the vessel upon receipt of your amendment advice.

5. We demand prompt delivery; otherwise we will have to cancel the order as per the contract.

6. Something unexpected compels us to seek your cooperation by advancing shipment of the goods under Order No. 234 from October to September.

7. As our users are in urgent need of the consignment, please get the goods dispatched within the stipulated time.

8. We hope the goods can reach the port of destination smoothly to meet with your requirements.

9. We greatly regret the delay, which has been due to circumstance beyond our control.

10. We would like to remind you that the goods should be shipped by October

20th as stipulated in the L/C; if not, you should be liable for any loss that might be caused by the delay of shipment.

Ⅲ. Translate the following letter into Chinese.

敬启者:

我们已收到贵方 8 月 10 日的来信,信中要求我们将自行车订单中的装运时间提前至 8 月 20 日。

一收到来信,我们立刻与装运代理联系。但很遗憾,他们告诉我们,对于贵方的订单,8 月份舱位不够。如果贵方希望尽早装运,我们只能 8 月份装运 200 箱,其余的 9 月份装运。

请尽早告知贵方的意见。

谨上

Ⅳ. Translate the following letter into English.

Dear Sirs,

Re: Purchase Contract No. 123

We have received your letter dated June 25, asking for definite information of shipment of the subjected goods.

Due to the peak season of shipment, we ourselves are still waiting for a reply from the local shipping agents concerning the matter of space, and we are unable to give you any good news at the moment. However, we are doing our utmost to deliver the goods before the relative credit expires.

We regret for any inconvenience to you by the delay caused by the shortage of shipping space. We expect to let you know by fax the result of our efforts in the next few days.

Yours sincerely,

Ⅴ. Letter writing.

Dear Sirs,

Thank you for your L/C No. 345 for 2,000 pieces of men's shirts. As stipulated in the L/C, shipment should be effected during July in one lot. However our forwarding agent informed us yesterday that shipping space on S. S. Peace nominated by you was insufficient. So it is hard for us to effect shipment in one lot. As you desire punctual shipment, we can only effect partial shipment of 1,000 pieces per S. S. Peace and the rest per S. S. Sunshine. Since this is the best arrangement we can propose, we hope it will meet with your approval.

Should you find the new arrangement acceptable, please telex an amendment to the concerned L/C allowing us to effect partial shipment.

We await your prompt reply so that we can expedite delivery.

Yours sincerely,

Chapter 11

Ⅰ. Fill in the blanks with the appropriate words.

As, between, for, of, on, to, against, for, against, by, accordingly, effect, without, if

Ⅱ. Translate the following sentences into Chinese.

1. 我们希望贵方能代我方为上述货物投保。

2. 对以 FOB 达成的交易,保险应由买方办理。

3. 我们很想知道贵方是否为葡萄酒投保一切险。

4. 若未明确指示,我们将按惯常为贵方订单投保。

5. 一旦完成所有手续我们将获得保险单。

6. 我们注意到贵方希望我们为这批货物投保金额为发票价值 110% 的保险,我们对此给予应有的关注。

7. 贵方能否告知我们是否能为这批货物投保一切险,如果能,什么条款?

8. 请在本月 24 日前将保单和签字过的副本寄交我方,费用记我方青岛分公司的账户。

9. 若客户没有特别指示,我们一般为货物投保水渍险和战争险。

10. 我们将根据合同坚持我们通常的做法,并殷切地希望这不会影响我们未来的业务关系。

Ⅲ. Translate the following sentences into English.

1. We will cover insurance on 100 metric tons of wool for 110% of the invoice value against All Risks.

2. Please note that insurance has been covered only against FPA and breakage.

If coverage against other risks is required, the extra premium involved would be for your account.

3. Please remark that insurance has been covered against WA as per warehouse-to-warehouse clauses valid within fifteen days.

4. Insurance should be covered for 110% of our CIF value. If coverage against other risks is required, please let us know in advance and extra premium is for the buyer's account.

5. Please take out insurance as requested. Meanwhile we are awaiting your shipping advice.

6. Premium for breakage is 5%. If you desire to cover breakage, we will arrange it on your behalf.

7. Your request for insurance to be covered up to the inland city can be accepted on condition that such extra premium is for your account.

8. The premium varies with the nature of the goods, the coverage and the port of destination.

9. For any issue about insurance please do not hesitate to contact us. We will spare no effort to serve you.

10. For the sake of safety, we recommend you to cover insurance for shipment against All Risks and War Risk.

Ⅳ. Translate the following letter into Chinese.

敬启者:

关于第 214 号售货合同项下的 4 000 箱铁钉,我们很高兴地告知贵方,我们已通过中国银行纽约支行开出了第 213 号保兑的不可撤销的信用证,金额为 20 000 美元,有效期至 5 月 15 日。

请注意上述商品将在 5 月 15 日前装运,投保一切险,保险金额为发票价值的 130%。我们知道,按照通常的做法,贵方只为货物投保发票价值的 110%,额外保险的保费由我们承担。

请按我们的要求投保,期待贵方的装船通知。

谨上

V. Translate the following letter into English.

Dear Sirs,

We are writing to you in reply to your letter of September 4 regarding insurance.

Your customer's request for insurance coverage up to the inland city is acceptable on condition that such extra premium is for his account.

We cannot grant your insurance coverage for 150% of the invoice value, because the contract stipulates that insurance is to be covered for 110% of invoice value.

We trust the above information serves your purpose. Meanwhile we await your reply.

Yours faithfully,

VI. Letter writing.

Dear Sirs,

We have pleasure in informing you that we have booked S. S. Peace, which is scheduled to sail for New York on or about July 7, 2025 to carry 3,000 pieces of men's shirts with a total invoice value of US $ 70,500. As per the sales contract, you should insure the goods against All Risks for the total invoice value plus 10%.

We hope you will find the above helpful.

Yours sincerely,

Chapter 12

I. Translate the following sentences into Chinese.

1. 由于贵方在交货上的严重延误,我们通知贵方取消我们的订单。

2. 由于我们之间有良好的关系,如果贵方能够降价 20%,我们打算接受这批货物。

3. 很遗憾,我方不得不投诉贵方迟交我方 5 月 12 日所订货物。正如贵方所知,准时装运对我方来说非常重要。

4. 我方同意贵方的投诉,并对由此给贵方造成的不便表示歉意。下周将把替换的商品发给贵方。

5. 所交货物未达到样品的质量标准:花样不匀,颜色有差异。

6. 商品的劣质给我们带来相当的不便,我们难以处理。

7. 很遗憾,开箱后我们发现里面装的是完全不同的商品。我们猜测哪儿出错了,箱子里装的是其他订单的商品。

8. 我们很遗憾地告知贵方产品与样品间的色差是正常的、在允许范围内的,因此,贵方所提的索赔是不合实际的。

9. 鉴于商品的高品质,很遗憾我们不能降价。如果贵方不能接受,我们同意托收付款方式。

10. 由于过期两个多月了,我们不太可能同意贵方的索赔要求。

Ⅱ. Translate the following sentences into English.

1. It is just and fair to propose a reduction of 30% in the contractual price; otherwise, the buyer has the right to reject the goods and lodge a claim according to the stipulations of the contract.

2. Upon examination, we found that many of the goods were severely damaged, though the cases themselves show no trace of damage.

3. As the quality of the goods is far from that stipulated in the contract, we regret that we can do nothing but refund them.

4. It is apparent that the damage was caused by improper packing. Before we deliver the goods to our clients we have to repack. Therefore we lodge a claim against you for compensation of the extra expenses thereof.

5. The deviation between the products and the samples is normal and permissible; therefore, the compensation claimed is impractical.

6. The goods were in perfect condition on leaving our warehouse and the damage has evidently occurred in transit.

7. As the damage is apparently due to rough handling in transit, it is only appropriate for you to file your claim with the insurance company concerned.

8. We are improving our packing as requested and hope the next shipment can comply with your requirement.

9. This is the maximum concession we can make. Should you not agree to accept our proposal, we would like to submit the case to arbitration.

10. As your claim does not comply with the result of our experiment, we ask you to re-inspect them to certify whether it is reasonable for you to lodge a claim

against us.

Ⅲ. Translate the following letter into Chinese.

敬启者：

谢谢来信通知我们所交运的货物（发票号为678）受到损坏。

从我们双方以往的交易中贵方应当了解，这次事件纯属偶然。但我们还是为给贵方造成的麻烦深表歉意。

请将所有的货物退还，我们将请船运公司来检查损失，以便他们安排赔偿。这件事不必麻烦我们的保险公司。

如果贵方还希望我们根据456号订单再次运货，请通知我们。我们仍有该批服装的存货，并且能于两周内发货。

谨上

Ⅳ. Translate the following letter into English.

Dear Sirs,

Re: Our Order No. 234

We thank you for the shipment of camping tents under our Order No. 234, which arrived yesterday and over which we are filing a complaint.

The boxes in which the camping tents were packed were damaged, and looked as if they had been broken open in transit. From your invoice No. 678 we estimate that twenty tents as well as a number of accessory lights have been stolen to the value of about US $ 3,200. The tents in the damaged boxes will not be able to be sold as new articles in our outlets here, since they were all crushed or stained as a result of the in-transit botching.

As the deal was on CIF basis and the forwarding company was your agent, we suggest you contact them with regard to compensation. You will find a list of the damaged and missing articles attached, and the consignment will be put aside until we receive your instructions.

Yours sincerely,

Ⅴ. Letter writing.

Dear Sirs,

We have recently received a lot of complaints from our customers about your men's shirt.

We examined some of the goods complained about and found they clearly do not match the samples you supplied. We are therefore writing to ask you to reduce the price by 4%.

We trust you will promptly settle this claim.

Yours faithfully,

Chapter 13

Ⅰ. Translate the following letter into English.

Dear Mr. Smith,

I would like to convey my heartiest congratulations to you on your promotion to the manager of the East China Sea Trading Company. No doubt, you have been one of the most diligent in the company in the past few years. My fellows and I are delighted that the service you have given to your company as well as your ability and contributions should at last have been rewarded in this way.

I believe this promotion will give you good opportunities to realize your ambitions. I send you my sincere wishes for the future.

Yours sincerely,

Ⅱ. Translate the following letter into Chinese.

亲爱的史密斯先生:

由于您的帮助,这次会议非常成功,非常感谢。

您的演讲是深刻的,由于它,大家对有关国际贸易未来的发展展开了激烈的辩论。我相信,您的演讲一定让与会者们都受益匪浅。

再次对您的参会及对会议成功所发挥的关键作用表示感谢!

谨上

References
参考文献

[1]董晓波. 国际贸易英语函电[M]. 北京:清华大学出版社,2010.

[2]任东红. 国际商务函电[M]. 北京:清华大学出版社,2012.

[3]仲鑫. 外贸函电[M]. 北京:机械工业出版社,2010.

[4]杨乐梅. 商务英语函电及单证[M]. 天津:南开大学出版社,2009.

[5]盛美娟. 商务英语函电[M]. 武汉:华中科技大学出版社,2009.

[6]兰天. 外贸英语函电[M]. 大连:东北财经大学出版社,2011.

[7]孙平. 新编商务函电[M]. 北京:清华大学出版社,2010.

[8]刘超先. 外贸英语单证与函电[M]. 上海:复旦大学出版社,2008.

[9]喆儒. 现代国际商务函电[M]. 北京:人民邮电出版社,2011.

[10]王虹. 外贸英语函电[M]. 北京:清华大学出版社,2009.

[11]赵银德. 外贸函电[M]. 北京:机械工业出版社,2010.

[12]帅建林. 国际贸易实务(英文版)[M]. 北京:对外经济贸易大学出版社,2012.

[13]王健. 国际贸易实务实训模拟教程[M]. 北京:对外经济贸易大学出版社,2012.

[14]王美玲. 外贸函电[M]. 北京:机械工业出版社,2013.

[15]王素清. 国际商务写作教程[M]. 北京:对外经济贸易大学出版社,1995.

[16]全国国际商务专业人员职业资格考试用书编委会. 国际商务英语[M]. 北京:中国商务出版社,2008.

[17]毅冰. 十天搞定外贸函电(白金版)[M]. 北京:中国海关出版社,2019.